NOW YOU'RE COOKING!

Over 80 Quick and Easy Recipes When You Don't Want to Eat Out

Charlene Frazier

MEGA DREAMS
ENTERPRISES, LLC
ESTABLISHED 2022

Now You're Cooking
Over 80 Quick & Easy Recipes When You Don't Want to Eat Out
Charlene Frazier

Published by Mega Dreams Enterprises LLC, Raleigh, NC
Copyright ©2024 Charlene Frazier
All rights reserved.

No part of this publication may be reproduced, stored in a retrieval system, or transmitted in any form or by any means, electronic, mechanical, photocopying, recording, scanning, or otherwise, except as permitted under Section 107 or 108 of the 1976 United States Copyright Act, without the prior written permission of the Publisher. Requests to the Publisher for permission should be addressed to Permissions Department, Mega Dreams Enterprises LLC info@megadreamsenterprises.com

Limit of Liability/Disclaimer of Warranty: While the publisher and author have used their best efforts in preparing this book, they make no representations or warranties with respect to the accuracy or completeness of the contents of this book and specifically disclaim any implied warranties of merchantability or fitness for a particular purpose. No warranty may be created or extended by sales representatives or written sales materials. The advice and strategies contained herein may not be suitable for your situation. You should consult with a professional where appropriate. Neither the publisher nor the author shall be liable for any loss of profit or any other commercial damages, including but not limited to special, incidental, consequential, or other damages.

The product information and advice provided (in this book) are intended for general informational purposes only. The author and publisher of this book have made every effort to ensure that the content is accurate and up-to-date at the time of publication. However, they make no representations or warranties of any kind, express or implied, about the completeness, accuracy, reliability, suitability, or availability of the information, products, or services contained in this book for any purpose.

Cover and Interior Design is a compilation of input from many experts, including,

Enrica Berto; fizart_gallary; Connect Branding + Marketing

Project Management and Final Design: Davis Creative, LLC / DavisCreativePublishing.com

Copyeditor: Helen Martineau, https://www.helenmartineauediting.com/

Library of Congress Cataloging-in-Publication Data

Names: Frazier, Charlene, author.

Title: Now you're cooking! : over 80 quick and easy recipes when you don't want to eat out / Charlene Frazier.

Description: Raleigh, NC : Mega Dreams Enterprises LLC, [2024] | Includes index.

Identifiers: ISBN: 979-8-9859627-0-3 (paperback) | 979-8-9859627-1-0 (hardback) | 979-8-9859627-2-7 (ebook) | LCCN: 2024903689

Subjects: LCSH: Quick and easy cooking. | LCGFT: Cookbooks. | BISAC: COOKING / General. | COOKING / Regional & Cultural / American / General. | COOKING / Courses & Dishes / General.

Classification: LCC: TX833.5 .F73 2024 | DDC: 641.555--dc23

2024

ATTENTION CORPORATIONS, UNIVERSITIES, COLLEGES AND PROFESSIONAL ORGANIZATIONS: Quantity discounts are available on bulk purchases of this book for educational, gift purposes, or as premiums for increasing magazine subscriptions or renewals. Special books or book excerpts can also be created to fit specific needs. For information, please contact Charlene Frazier, Mega Dreams Enterprises LLC, info@megadreamsenterprises.com https://megadreamsenterprises.com

Interior photography on pages 9, 13, 25, 31, 37, 45, 71, 75, 77, 79, 81, 89, 91, 95, 97, 99, 101, 103, 113, 115, 119, 126, 135, 139, 151, and 157 by Stephen Mallin of Mallin Photography of NC, Inc.

Food stylist: Dawn Longobardo

Cover and additional photography on pages 10, 18, 29, 35, 39, 55, 57, 59, 65, 67, 117, 129, 133, 141, 143, 145, and 147 by Allen Thompson of Ag Photography

Food stylists: Andre and Lethia Owens

Additional photography on page 8 by Dr. Evisha Ford Brown

Hair: Lethia Owens (cover) and Shervon Kee Melvin

Makeup: Carley Quinn (cover) and Nicole Melvin

Mega Dreams Enterprises, LLC

Table of Contents

Acknowledgements 5
Preface 6
Introduction 7
Foreword 8
About the Author 9
A Well-Stocked Kitchen 10
Basic Equipment 11
Nice to Have 11
Pantry Items 12
Fridge Items 12
Measurements and Equivalents............ 14
Cooking 101 15
Basic Cooking Terms............................... 15
Meal Planning 17
Sample Week #1 Menu for two people. 19
Sample Week #2 Menu for two people. 24
Breakfast 26
Frisky Frittata 27
Mrs. Hopson's Breakfast Pie 28
Banana Pudding Smoothie 30
Strawberry Banana Smoothie 32
Breakfast Muffins 33
Country Sausage Egg Bites..................... 34
Turkey Breakfast Sausage 36
Mini Toaster Waffles............................... 38
Avocado Toast 40
Snacks & Appetizers 41
Parmesan-Ranch Potato Chips............... 42
Thanksgiving Crescent Rolls................... 43
Crab Dip 44
Corn and Black Bean Relish 46
Turkey Pepperoni and Sausage Pizza Pockets... 47

Snickerdoodle Smoothie........................... 48
Soups & Salads (& a Sandwich)...............49
Chicken Noodle Soup 50
Chicken Tortilla Soup 51
Tasty Turkey Chili...................................... 52
Cucumber Salad 53
Sweet Potato and Apple Bisque............. 54
Tomato Soup 56
Grilled Cheese Sandwich 58
Savory Broccoli Salad............................... 60
Avocado Ranch Dressing 61
Apple Pecan Chicken Salad..................... 62
Apple and Cabbage Slaw......................... 63
Southwest Chicken Salad 64
Chicken Salad in Tomato Shells 66
Baked Tomato Shells................................ 68
Poultry..69
Doritos-Crusted Chicken Tenders........... 70
Southwestern Dipping Sauce 72
Hot Chicken Salad.................................... 73
Chicken Pot Pie 74
Baked Turkey Wings 76
Amazing Italian Stuffed Peppers............. 78
Chicken Parmesan 80
Baked Chicken Breasts............................. 82
Baked Chicken Thighs with Balsamic Glaze 83
Air-Fried Lemon Pepper Chicken Wings. 84
Seafood..85
Tuna Salad 86
Seafood Pot Pie 87
Air-Fried Salmon Patties.......................... 88
Tuna Pasta 90

Side Dishes 92
  Baked Potatoes 93
  Green Beans with Almonds 94
  Sautéed Mushrooms and Spinach 96
  Flava Beans 98
  Steamed Zucchini and Yellow Squash . 100
  Easy Mac and Cheese 102
  Honey-Butter Corn Muffins 104
  Smoky Greens 105
  Roasted Asparagus 106
  Yellow Rice 107
  Sautéed Cabbage 108

Mother Dear, Can We Get Outside Food? 109
  Oreo Milkshake 110
  Air-Fried Sweet Potato Fries 111
  McDowell's Breakfast Burrito 112
  Southwestern Egg Rolls 114
  Air-Fried French Fries 116
  Shrimp Teriyaki Stir-Fry 118
  Air-Fried Shrimp Hushpuppies 120
  Shrimp Fried Rice 121

Time for a Kickback!
Let's Throw a Casual Dinner Party 122
  Menu 122
  Work Plan 122
  One month to three weeks ahead 122
  Two to three weeks ahead 123
  One week ahead 123
  Three days before party 123
  One day before party 123
  Two hours before guests arrive 124
  One hour before guests arrive 124
  Thirty minutes before guests arrive 124
  Fifteen minutes before 124
  Just before sitting down to dinner 124
  While enjoying the soup 124
  While enjoying dinner 125
  Dinner Party Grocery List 125
  Herbed Cream Cheese Crescent Rolls 127
  Moscato Punch 128
  French Onion Soup 130
  Mixed Greens with Balsamic
  Vinaigrette 131
  Scalloped Potatoes 132
  Simply Delicious Apple Dump Cake 134
  Roasted Chicken Breasts with
  Lemon-Basil Sauce 136

Charlene's Favorites 137
  Chicken Liver Pâté 138
  Air-Fried Chicken Livers 140
  Lasagna 142
  Sexy Meatloaf with Brown Sugar Glaze 144
  Charlene's Front Porch Lemonade 146
  Spiced Hot Chocolate 148

Desserts 149
  Banana Rum Cake 150
  7Up Pound Cake 152
  Sweet Potato Pie 153
  Peanut Butter Oatmeal Bars 154
  Chocolate-Dipped Oatmeal Cookies . 155
  Bourbon Sea Salt Caramel Turtles 156

Family Recipes 157
  Mother Frazier's Brown Sugar
  Pound Cake 157

Resources 162

Index 163

Acknowledgements

First and foremost, I give thanks to God for His showers of blessings and grace throughout the years it has taken to complete this book successfully.

I would like to express my deep and sincere gratitude to the following people who helped to make this cookbook possible:

My late grandmother Rutha Lee Frazier and my mother, Betty Geiger Frazier, for allowing me to hang out in their kitchens and showing me how to show love through food.

Andre and Lethia Owens. I don't know where to start. Thank you for stepping in whenever there was a need: opening your home to me, cooking, washing dishes, styling food, picking up clothes, making sure my hair was right, holding me accountable, pushing me in front of the camera. I love you guys!

Chef Jerome Brown, my friend and mentor. Thank you for supporting, encouraging, and challenging me. I can't thank you enough.

Jade and Lisa Paden, for allowing chaos into their home. The pictures turned out great! I am eternally grateful.

My photographers Allen Thompson and Stephen Mallin; Stephen's assistant, Mark Metro; my food stylist, Dawn Longobardo; and Dawn's assistant, Athina Sgambati. Thank you for bringing my recipes to life in this book. Your work made all the difference.

My editor, Helen Martineau, words cannot express how much you have meant to this project. Thank you for your patience and for making sure my recipes make sense.

Tisha Turner, one of my first office mates at IBM and my dear friend, thank you for your encouragement and support.

My siblings, Barbara, Yelberton, and Charles. Thank you all for your encouragement and support. Special thanks to Yelberton for inspiring the dump cake recipe.

Dr. Leslie King Gipson, my oldest and dearest friend, thank you for your encouragement.

My book coach, Tressa Smallwood, for teaching me the ins and outs of publishing my first book.

Jack and Cathy Davis. Thank you for making sure I have dotted all the I's and crossed all the t's needed to get this book released. I could not have released this book without the two of you.

Game Changers Mastermind Retreat in Dubai. Thank you all for your ideas, encouragement, and support.

All the recipe and taste testers. There are too many to list here, but you know who you are. Well, I would be remiss if I didn't shout out my favorite guinea pigs Cynthia Bernard and Rodney and Teresa Caldwell. Thank you all for your willingness to try my creations and provide honest feedback.

Preface

Why did I write a cookbook? My desire to write a cookbook came from my own culinary journey: my love of food, memories of cooking with my mother and grandmother, the excitement I feel when trying out new dishes from my cookbook collection and discovering new dishes and flavor combinations while dining out. Could I really write a cookbook? Even though it has been a goal of mine for years, I had to overcome my own insecurities about my qualifications. I didn't attend culinary school. Was I capable? No one would see me as an expert. But I came to realize that I am good at what I do; I haven't killed anyone with my cooking, and my friends and family enjoy the meals I prepare. Growing up, I trained under my grandmother, staying in the kitchen with her for hours whenever I visited while she prepared dishes at the kitchen table. It was my job to grab ingredients and hand them to her. I watched and asked questions. My mother, a retired librarian, started my fascination with cookbooks because of her cookbook collection. Now I actually read the cookbooks in my own collection as though they were novels, thinking of ways to create my own version of a recipe. It has taken me five years to overcome my insecurities and fear, to learn the process of self-publishing a cookbook, and to gather the funds needed for each phase.

What did I want to accomplish with this cookbook?

- I wanted my first cookbook to be a collection of recipes that are inexpensive and easy to make and will result in food that's just as satisfying and tasty as what you might enjoy outside of the home. A lot of my recipes are inspired by my favorite restaurant dishes.

- My goal was to create a collection of recipes that would allow you to build a weekly menu so you're not always forced to eat out.

- This book was created to help you learn how to cook for yourself.

- How many of you have ever shopped for groceries over the weekend, convincing yourself that you're going to save money during the week by cooking dinner for yourself, only to end up throwing ingredients in the trash days later because something in the fridge smells bad? Life got in the way. You ended up working too late and getting takeout on the way home or taking your friends or coworkers up on their offer to join them for a late dinner. I know I'm not the only one who has done that. Imagine not having the energy to do what you love doing the most at the end of the day; that was me. I decided to write a cookbook that emphasizes meal planning and prep to increase my chances of cooking for myself while reducing the likelihood of spoiled groceries.

Cooking can be a way to express your creativity and show love to your friends and family. I hope this helps you to experiment and become more comfortable in the kitchen. It might not make you an expert, but it will, I hope, inspire you to learn your way around the kitchen and cook more. We should all strive to be lifelong culinary students, eager to learn about the latest cooking techniques, new and interesting flavor combinations, and appliances that will help us prepare great home-cooked meals. I completed my first cookbook! This comes from my heart and my kitchen with the right portions of taste and time.

Introduction

Why cook for yourself?

- You know what you're eating. When you eat out, you really can't be sure what is in the food you're buying. Cooking your own food ensures you're not ingesting preservatives or ingredients that you may not want (think allergies, aversions, and dietary restrictions). For example, if you don't like spicy foods, you can omit ingredients like cayenne pepper or add less than the amount specified in a recipe. Likewise, you can always incorporate any partialities you may have: If you're into heat, you can substitute spicy canned tomatoes for regular ones. Unless you already know that you're allergic to or dislike a particular ingredient in a recipe, it is best to follow it as written the first time you make it, then tweak it to make it your own the next time.

- It will unleash your creativity. Once you become comfortable with cooking, you will want to try different cuisines and seasonings. You may eventually use these or other recipes as a base to create your own.

- It is much easier to measure and control portion sizes. Eating out too much can cause weight gain. Restaurants typically provide portion sizes that are two or three times the recommended portion. Cooking at home makes it easy to divide food into the recommended servings provided in recipes. It is much harder to overeat when you separate food into individual servings when you prepare it and store them in the fridge or freezer to eat later.

- You can save money. According to the US Bureau of Labor Statistics, the average American household spends an average of $3,526 per year on dining out. You can save roughly half that amount by planning and cooking your meals at home. We have all been guilty of throwing out unused groceries and takeout. The average household of four wastes $1,500 per year throwing out food. Spend four to six hours per week creating healthy meals that you can package for portion control and consume immediately or up to two weeks later.

- You can learn a skill that will feed you for life (pun intended). Snowed in? Car in the shop? Quarantined? Upcoming hospital stay? As long as you can stock your pantry and fridge with groceries, there is no reason to ever feel hangry (i.e., angry or cranky because you're hungry).

- If you have a family, cooking at home is a great way to spend quality time together. Not only will everyone eat better and become more aware of what they're eating, you will also inadvertently teach your kids (girls AND boys) a skill that will serve them when they move out on their own. They will cherish favorite recipes and pass them on to their children.

- If you're single, cooking at home is a great way to spend quality time with friends. Consider hosting a cooking party where you and your friends prepare a variety of meals and split the cost of ingredients. You could also share a membership to one of those big-box stores for additional savings.

Foreword

"Your hospitality shows me that you care"
— Lyrics from a song by Frankie Beverly and Maze

Chef Charlene is an amazing soul. From the moment I met her, I could hear the passion that she has for cooking. With over 500 cookbooks in her collection, she's obtained knowledge that allows her to display her passion to her loved ones and closest friends.

I remember the day I finally tasted her Apple Dump Cake (page 134); I could taste the love in every bite. It was my first time having such a simply delicious and amazing dessert. But it didn't stop there, the Front Porch Lemonade (page 146) was everything I ever wanted lemonade to be.

I invite you to sit back, loosen your top button, and leave your diet on the shelf. Get your kitchen ready for cooking 101. Prepare your taste buds for excitement. After your guests arrive and the first taste is experienced, they will all say, "Now you're cooking!"

Charlene, I applaud you, I'm proud of you, and I can't wait to try a dish from your cookbook!

Chef Jerome Brown aka Chef Rome

Food Network's Extreme Chef

Cookbook author, Chef to the Stars

About the Author

I am affectionately known as Chef Charlene. My passion for culinary arts began when I was a little girl helping my mother and grandmother bake cakes, brownies, and cookies. Whenever I heard the mixer start, I would stop whatever I was doing to run into the kitchen so I could lick the bowl. When I was old enough, they taught me how to bake, which ignited my passion for cooking. I eventually graduated from using my Easy Bake oven to a real oven! When I grew older, I became responsible for baking cookies to leave out for Santa.

During my high school days in Albany, Georgia, I became interested in computer science when I took a BASIC programming class. I completed my bachelor's degree in computer science at Albany State College (now Albany State University), where I pledged Alpha Kappa Alpha sorority. I also obtained my master's degree in computer science from Clark Atlanta University.

During these journeys, I began to prepare my meals and follow a budget for groceries, thus building my cooking and cuisine knowledge. After my master's, I was recruited by IBM and began my career as a software tester in Boca Raton, Florida. I was exposed to lots of seafood restaurants in South Florida and learned to try and appreciate new dishes. Shortly after moving to Florida, I transferred to Austin, Texas, where I was offered many different types of cuisine. I learned about brisket for the first time and a different style of barbecue from what I grew up enjoying. In the late nineties, I transferred to Research Triangle Park, North Carolina and transitioned to software development and eventually project management. It was here that I learned yet another style of barbecue and continued to try new dishes.

Over the years, I collected over 500 cookbooks. I took a few culinary classes to learn necessary cooking skills as well as the responsibilities of a personal chef. As a chef, I enjoy discovering new flavor combinations and exploring new cooking techniques. In 2018, after twenty-three years at IBM, a corporate layoff allowed me to further develop my love of cooking. In 2020 I joined HCLTech as a project manager in Cary, North Carolina but my passion for the culinary arts remained. After a second layoff in 2024 I realized I needed to pursue my passion full time.

On a personal level, I love traveling and spending time with family and friends.

A Well-Stocked Kitchen

Here's the list of equipment that should be in every kitchen. However, if you don't have all these items, that doesn't mean you can't cook. My recipes will offer suggestions for alternative equipment, if practical, for those on a budget, and you can gradually collect the items over time.

Mandoline

Basic Equipment

- Chef's knife
- Measuring spoons
- Can opener
- Paring knife
- Measuring cups
- Whisk
- 10-inch nonstick skillet
- 12-inch nonstick skillet
- 3- or 4-quart saucepan
- 6-quart stockpot
- Mini-muffin pan
- 6-cup muffin pan
- Baking sheet
- 8-inch square baking dish
- 13x9-inch baking pan
- 1.5-quart casserole dish
- Mixing bowls
- Cutting boards
- Colander
- Strainer
- High-speed blender
- Hand mixer
- Vegetable peeler

Nice to Have

- Large pitcher
- Mandoline
- Potato ricer
- Microplane grater set
- Vegetable brush
- Vegetable chopper
- French fry cutter
- Steamer basket
- Pasta pot with insert
- Deep pie dish
- Shallow pie dish
- Bundt pan
- Meatloaf pan
- 9x5-inch loaf pan
- 12-cup muffin pan
- Lasagna pan
- Rimmed baking pan
- Wire cooling rack
- Oven liner
- Kitchen scale
- Food processor
- Rice cooker
- Stand mixer
- Bread machine
- Air fryer
- Mini-waffle maker
- Vacuum sealer
- Dredging pans (3)
- Large punch bowl
- Rice-washing bowl
- Souper Cubes
- Shape + Store container
- Fine-mesh strainer
- Sifter

Again, if you don't have everything on this list, that doesn't mean you can't cook. This is a list of commonly used items to make the recipes in this book.

Pantry Items

- Sea salt
- Kosher salt
- Black pepper
- Ground cinnamon
- Ground nutmeg
- Ground cumin
- Red pepper flakes
- Paprika
- Dried oregano
- Dried dill
- Dried rosemary
- Dried thyme
- Dried basil
- Dried tarragon
- Onion powder
- Garlic powder
- Hidden Valley Ranch dressing mix
- Extra-virgin olive oil
- Worcestershire sauce
- Low-sodium soy sauce
- Balsamic vinegar
- Vanilla extract
- Cornstarch
- All-purpose flour
- Sugar
- Light brown sugar
- Yellow onions
- Garlic cloves
- Sweet onions
- Red onions
- Russet potatoes
- Pecans
- Brown rice
- Jasmine rice
- Ro-Tel diced tomatoes
- Baker's Joy cooking spray
- Parchment paper
- Silpat mat

Fridge Items

- Mayonnaise
- Dijon mustard
- Salad dressing
- Better Than Bouillon chicken base
- Better Than Bouillon vegetable base
- Minced garlic
- Baby bella mushrooms
- Baby spinach
- Lettuce
- Bell peppers
- Cabbage
- Cucumbers
- Carrots
- Celery
- Bananas
- Lemons
- Limes
- Boneless skinless chicken breasts
- Eggs
- Unsalted butter
- Whole milk
- American cheese slices
- Shredded cheddar cheese
- Grated Parmesan cheese
- Shredded mozzarella cheese

Equipment: crock with utensils, cutting boards, high-speed blender, food processor, vacuum sealer, chef's knife, bread knife, paring knife, hand mixer

Now You're Cooking!

Measurements and Equivalents:

(Tbsp = tablespoon; tsp = teaspoon)

Liquid and dry ingredients:

Dash = 1/8 tsp
1 Tbsp = 3 tsp
4 Tbsp = ¼ cup = 2 fl oz
5 1/3 Tbsp = ⅓ cup
16 Tbsp = 1 cup = 8 fl oz
2 cups = 1 pint = 16 fl oz
4 cups = 1 quart = 2 pints = 32 fl oz
16 cups = 1 gallon = 4 quarts = 8 pints = 128 fl oz

Butter:

1 Tbsp = ⅛ stick = 0.5 oz = 15 g
2 Tbsp = ¼ stick = 1 oz = 30 g
4 tbsp = ½ stick = ¼ cup = 2 oz = 60 g
8 Tbsp = 1 stick = ½ cup = 4 oz = 115 g
16 Tbsp = 2 sticks = 1 cup = 8 oz = 225 g
32 Tbsp = 4 sticks = 2 cups = 16 oz = 1 lb = 450 g

Substitutions

2 Tbsp butter = 1 oz butter
Juice of 1 lemon = 3 Tbsp lemon juice
1 cup buttermilk = 1 cup whole milk + 1 Tbsp vinegar or 1 Tbsp lemon juice
2 egg whites = 1 whole egg
8 egg whites = 1 cup egg whites
1 medium onion = ¼ cup dried minced onion

Standards Used in Most Recipes (unless otherwise noted)

Egg = Large egg
Milk = Whole milk
Sugar = Granulated sugar
Brown sugar = Light brown sugar
Flour = All-purpose flour
1 cup flour, sifted ≠ 1 cup sifted flour
1 cup flour, sifted = measure the flour first, then sift
1 cup sifted flour = sift the flour first, then measure

Cooking 101

Basic Cooking Terms

These are some terms that you will need to know to become more comfortable cooking and to create your own recipes. Many of the terms or concepts mentioned here are included in recipes in this book.

- **Asian trinity** – the combination of ginger, garlic, and scallions in Chinese cooking. It is sometimes referred to as Chinese mirepoix.

- **Broth** – a seasoned cooking liquid made from chicken, beef, fish, or vegetables. It is simmered for up to two hours. Broth can be used as the base for soups and as a water replacement for rice, pasta, or potatoes. It should be noted that bone broth is actually a type of stock. It is made from bones and connective tissue and is simmered for up to forty-eight hours. It contains collagen protein, which is highly sought-after for its health and beauty benefits (e.g., strong hair and nails).

- **Dicing** – cutting vegetables into equal-sized cubes or dice. Cutting vegetables in this manner ensures even cooking and is more visually appealing.

- **Fond** – a French term that refers to the browned bits of food on the bottom of a pan that result from roasting or sautéing. Fond adds flavor to sauces. In order to incorporate them into a sauce, you would deglaze (clean the pan) by adding wine or water to the pan to loosen the bits and scraping them up with a spoon.

- **Holy trinity** – similar to a mirepoix, but it replaces carrots with bell peppers. The ratio is typically equal parts onions, celery, and bell peppers. This veggie combo is quite often found in Cajun and Caribbean cuisine.

- **Mirepoix** (MEER-pwa) – the combination of diced onions, carrots, and celery in French cooking. The ratio of vegetables is typically two parts onions, one part celery, and one part carrots. The vegetables are cooked on low heat in butter or oil (or a combination of the two). A mirepoix is the flavor foundation for many dishes including stocks, sauces, meat dishes, and beans.

- **Mise en place** (MEEZ-n-PLAHS) – a French cooking process that means "to put in place," i.e., gathering, prepping, and measuring all the ingredients prior to cooking. This reduces stress, allowing you to enjoy cooking.

- **Roux** (roo) – equal parts fat and flour cooked together as the base for a sauce.

- **Sautéing** (saw-TEY-ing) – cooking quickly over relatively high heat using very little oil or fat.

- **Soffritto** (sew-FREE-toe) – also very similar to a mirepoix in that it consists of diced onions, carrots, and celery. Soffritto in Italian means "fried slowly." The vegetables are cooked in butter, oil, or pork fat until golden brown. It is commonly the base for Italian sauces, soups, and stews. Many regions in Italy have their own preferences as to the ratios of vegetables as well as the number of ingredients that make up a soffritto. Some Italian restaurants have even been known to have their own secret soffritto recipes.

- **Sweating** – removing the moisture from vegetables. This can be accomplished by cooking the vegetables with a little oil in a covered skillet on low heat until soft or, for raw vegetables such as cucumbers and tomatoes, tossing them in a bowl with salt and letting them sit for 30–40 minutes.

- **Vinaigrette** (vinna-GRET) – a sauce whose traditional foundation is one part vinegar (apple cider vinegar, red wine vinegar, balsamic vinegar, etc.) to three parts oil. Adding herbs, garlic salt, pepper, honey, or mustard enhances its flavor. A vinaigrette is most commonly used as a salad dressing, but it makes a great marinade as well.

Meal Planning

You must take time to plan your meals in advance if you want to save time, energy, and money by cooking. Meal planning ensures that you aren't reheating the same meal for three consecutive days; otherwise, boredom will set in, and before you know it, you're ordering takeout. Order out enough times and you'll soon have to throw out food (money!) from your fridge. When you plan your weekly meals, you'll only need to go to the store once per week. Fewer visits to the store mean fewer chances to succumb to impulse buying.

Put some thought into it. Think about the favorite dishes you or your family members enjoy and try to incorporate them into the weekly menu. You can even get input from your family (if they aren't voting to have chicken nuggets and French fries every day). Are there days of the week that you will only have time to reheat prepared meals? Are there days of the week that will allow you to boil water for pasta to make a quick mac and cheese or noodles to go with the chicken Parmesan you have in the fridge? Perhaps you can prepare shrimp fried rice on Saturday night since your daughter, who is allergic to shellfish, will be attending a slumber party that night.

Review each recipe you've chosen for the week and create a shopping list that includes the necessary ingredients. As you're choosing the recipes, try to include those that will require the same perishable ingredients. For years I would purchase a carton of buttermilk to use roughly one cup to make a red velvet cake, and I'd let the container sit in the fridge until it was time to throw it out. I later learned that I could marinate chicken pieces in buttermilk to make them more tender. Planning eliminates waste.

Gather tools and equipment to ensure success.

1. Download mobile apps to help you save time and money. Flipp, an all-in-one shopping app, lets you digitally browse weekly circulars, create a shopping list while looking for deals on each item, and load coupons to your loyalty cards. If Flipp indicates that chicken breasts are on sale this week, then it makes sense to select chicken recipes for this week's menu. You can even purchase additional chicken breasts to use much later (see step 4). Fetch Rewards, a grocery rebate app that is similar to Ibotta but easier to use, lets you scan your receipts from grocery stores, warehouse clubs, drugstores, and convenience stores to accumulate points that can be redeemed for gift cards.

2. Purchase good containers to store your food properly. Select storage containers that are airtight and can be safely used in a microwave or stored in a freezer. Glass containers are preferred because they don't stain and they can be used to reheat food in the oven, but BPA-free plastic is also acceptable. Never purchase containers that can't be put in the dishwasher (no one wants to spend time washing dishes unnecessarily). Good containers are essential for meal prep as well as for storing meals for the week. (More on this in step 3.)

3. Make soups ahead of time and freeze them. Products are available to easily freeze and retrieve portion-controlled servings. I personally like Souper Cubes because you can easily pop out a single

portion or as many portions as needed and keep the remaining soup in the freezer. Smoothies can also be made ahead of time, stored in a FroZip pouch, and placed in the freezer. It takes a few hours to thaw, so plan accordingly. Could you put a milkshake in a FroZip pouch? Yes, but why bother? It just seems wrong. Preparing milkshakes takes two seconds. If you want to skip the pouches and make a smoothie to consume the day of, you could create homemade smoothie freezer packs instead. Simply place all the ingredients (minus any protein powders you may want to add) in a resealable freezer bag then place it in the freezer. You can even add your almond milk to the bag—just freeze it in ice cube trays first: eight cubes equal one cup. When you're ready for a smoothie, grab your freezer pack out of the freezer and dump the contents, along with any protein powders you may want, into the blender.

4. Invest in a food vacuum sealer. The enemy of fresh food is air. Buying perishable food in bulk will generally save money, but if you end up throwing food away because it has gone bad before you can consume it, you're wasting money. Using a sealer like the FoodSaver will allow you to keep food up to five times longer. Purchase the larger package of chicken breasts, divide them into bags of three to four pieces, vacuum seal the bags, and place them in the freezer. The chicken will last two to three years in the freezer, if necessary. You can also buy cheese on sale and seal blocks of it for use later. The cheese will last four to eight months in the fridge if you seal it after every use vs. one to two weeks if stored in a Ziploc bag.

Where Do You Start?

Select the set of recipes you want to make for the week taking into account family members' preferences. Try to make sure everyone has at least one meal that they've requested. Your kid may not get chicken nuggets and fries every night, but you could agree to have that one night per week. I have added a sample menu for a couple here. It might appear daunting at first glance because there are twenty-nine recipes. The first week will be the most time-consuming because you're starting with no meals in the fridge. For this reason, you may want to divide your cooking into two or more days to prevent burnout. Going forward, you should have enough food in the freezer at the beginning of the week that you won't have to spend as much time in the kitchen.

Tomato Soup in Souper Cubes and Homemade Mini Waffles

Sample Week #1 Menu for two people

	Breakfast	**Lunch**	**Dinner**	**Snack**
Sunday	Mrs. Hopson's Breakfast Pie (page 28)	Dine out	Lasagna (page 142) Roasted Asparagus (page 106)	Southwestern Egg Rolls (page 114)
Monday	Strawberry-Banana Smoothie (page 32)	Grilled Cheese Sandwich (page 58) Tomato Soup (page 56)	Tasty Turkey Chili (page 52) Honey-Butter Corn Muffins (page 104)	Corn and Black Bean Relish with Tortilla Chips (page 46)
Tuesday	McDowell's Breakfast Burrito (page 112)	Hot Chicken Salad (page 73) Steamed Zucchini and Yellow Squash (page 100)	Air-Fried Lemon-Pepper Chicken Wings (page 84) Air-Fried Sweet Potato Fries (page 111) Apple and Cabbage Slaw (page 63)	Turkey Sausage and Pepperoni Pizza Pockets (page 47)
Wednesday	Banana Pudding Smoothie (page 30)	Apple Pecan Chicken Salad (page 62)	Baked Turkey Wings (page 76) Yellow Rice (page 107) Smoky Greens (page 105) Honey-Butter Corn Muffins (page 104)	Snickerdoodle Smoothie (page 48)
Thursday	Frisky Frittata (page 27)	Tuna Salad with crackers (page 86)	Lasagna (page 142) Steamed Zucchini and Yellow Squash (page 100)	Corn and Black Bean Relish with Tortilla Chips (page 46)
Friday	Breakfast Muffins (page 33)	Mrs. Hopson's Breakfast Pie (page 28)	Doritos-Crusted Chicken Tenders with Southwestern Dipping Sauce (page 70, 72) Air-Fried French Fries (page 116)	Oreo Milkshake (page 110)
Saturday	McDowell's Breakfast Burrito (page 112)	Tuna Salad with crackers (page 86)	Dine out	Doritos-Crusted Chicken Tenders with Southwestern Dipping Sauce (page 70)

Read the recipes you want to prepare in their entirety.

- Are you allergic to any of the ingredients? If it is a main ingredient, you obviously want to skip the recipe altogether, but if it is a small amount simply omit it. Perhaps checking the internet will yield a suitable substitute.

- Confirm which ingredients you already have in hand. Actually pull them out to make sure you have the quantities needed. I have had a few instances when I knew I had an ingredient only to discover I didn't have enough. For example, I knew cinnamon was in my pantry but when it was time to prepare the recipe, I realized I only had half a teaspoon when I needed one tablespoon.

- Confirm that you have all the equipment or alternative equipment needed to make the dish. Be willing to walk away from the recipe if you don't have the right equipment. As a child I can remember being excited that we had all the ingredients for a recipe in one of my mother's cookbooks only to discover a food processor was needed. Since we didn't have one and a rolling pin wouldn't yield satisfactory results, I had to skip the recipe.

- Confirm that you have set aside enough time to prepare the dish and do the necessary prep work. You don't want to start cooking one hour before you want dinner on the table only to realize you need to let the chicken marinate for thirty minutes or, in some cases, overnight. Eliminate any situation that will frustrate you and cause you to order a pizza to get food on the table quickly.

- Confirm that you understand all terms and steps in the recipes. Do your research before tackling a recipe to make sure you know what to do.

- Generate your grocery list. Depending on where you live you may have to order some ingredients online. If this is the case, you may want to select another recipe while you wait for that item to arrive.

Now it's time to head to the store.

Your Trip to the Grocery Store

- Now that you have reviewed your recipes and generated a grocery list, don't deviate from it once you get in the store! If you're not focused, you will inevitably pick up items that you don't need or won't use before they expire.

- Don't go to the store hungry. It will be very hard to resist putting junk food or prepared meals in your cart when you're starving. These items are usually pricey and unhealthy. Make sure that you have had a healthy meal or snack before you set foot in the store. This will also prevent snacking on the groceries on the way home, which could cause problems on cook day. For example, let's say you follow the sample menu above and buy the eight bananas needed to make two servings each of the Banana Pudding Smoothie and Strawberry Banana Smoothie. If you decide you want to eat a banana while sitting at a long traffic light, you won't have enough when you get home. Don't do it.

- Don't take the kids with you. A surefire way to blow your grocery budget is to bring family members along that are easily influenced by TV commercials selling sugary cereals or high-sodium snacks. Either you'll end up with a screaming child and long stares from fellow shoppers wondering why your child sounds like he/she is dying or whining/arguing with you, or you'll cave in and spend the extra money to appease your child. Save money and skip the drama by leaving your kids at home, if possible. Make sure to feed them first if you can't leave them at home.

- Get to know your grocery store manager and staff. If you're a regular customer at a store, it will be to your advantage to get to know the store manager and other employees (e.g., the butcher in the meat department). They may let you know about upcoming sales.

- Learn the layout of your grocery store. Time is money. If you're familiar with the layout of your store, you can group items in your grocery list based on where they are located so that you can quickly find the items you need. Some stores, like Publix, will let you compile a grocery list on their website that lists the aisle/section for each item.

- Sign up for your store's loyalty program. Additional sales are available to you if you're a member of your store's loyalty program. Some stores provide additional coupons for future use based on your purchases. But stay focused on your grocery list so that you don't end up spending more money to increase your rewards. If something is on sale that you don't really use or like, don't purchase it just because it is on sale.

- Pick the best day to grocery shop. So you don't feel as though you're spending a full workday grocery shopping and cooking, I suggest shopping on one day and prepping and cooking the next day. The best time to shop for groceries is one hour after your grocery store opens on Wednesday mornings. If your work schedule does not allow shopping in the middle of the week, the next best option is one hour after your grocery store opens on Saturday mornings.

If you truly don't have time to do your own shopping, you can try a grocery delivery service like Instacart. Most grocery stores offer a service that allows customers to shop online and have their groceries ready for them to be picked up at the store upon their scheduled arrival. I usually prefer selecting my own meat and produce, but I have used this service when I've been really busy. I love that I don't even have to get out of the car—I just park in a designated parking space for pickups and open the trunk.

Now that you have your groceries and they are put away, you're ready to start cooking. I typically get my groceries on a Saturday and cook on Sunday. As I said above, I don't recommend shopping and cooking on the same day; it's too much. But if you can't fit cooking into your schedule on other days, do what you have to do. As I mentioned earlier, the very first week you may have to cook over two or more days. Week number two won't be as daunting because you'll have leftovers from week number one to pull out of the freezer.

Sample Week #1 Prep and Cook Days
(for sample menu on page 19)

Prep Days

Friday (before week 1 starts)

Peel bananas for smoothies and place them in a resealable freezer bag. Store in freezer.

Saturday (before week 1 starts)

Boil eggs for tuna salad

Thursday

Cut potatoes for french fries and soak in water overnight

Cook Days

Friday (before week 1 starts)

- Tasty Turkey Chili (page 52)
- Honey-Butter Corn Muffins (page 104)
- Southwestern Egg Rolls (page 114)
- Brown rice for Breakfast Muffins (page 33)
- Yellow Rice (page 107)
- Mrs. Hopson's Breakfast Pie (page 28)

Saturday (before week 1 starts)

- Strawberry Banana Smoothie (page 32)
- Banana Pudding Smoothie (page 30)
- Snickerdoodle Smoothie (page 48)
- Frisky Frittata (page 27)
- Baked Turkey Wings (page 76)
- Tomato Soup (page 56)
- Turkey Sausage and Pepperoni Pizza Rolls (page 47)
- Breakfast Muffins (page 33)
- Lasagna (page 142)
- Smoky Greens (page 105)
- Steamed Zucchini and Yellow Squash (page 100)
- McDowell's Breakfast Burrito (page 112)

Sunday

- Roasted Asparagus (page 106)
- Grilled Cheese Sandwiches (page 58)

Monday

- Corn and Black Bean Relish (page 46)

Tuesday

- Air-Fried Lemon-Pepper Wings (page 84)
- Air-Fried Sweet Potato Fries (page 111)
- Apple and Cabbage Slaw (page 63)
- Apple Pecan Chicken Salad (page 62)

Wednesday

- Tuna Salad (page 86)

Friday

- Doritos-Crusted Chicken Tenders (page 70)
- Southwestern Dipping Sauce (page 72)
- Air-Fried French Fries (page 116)
- Oreo Milkshake (page 110)

Sample Week #2 Menu for two people
(start with leftovers from week #1)

	Breakfast	Lunch	Dinner	Snack
Sunday	Breakfast Muffins	Dine out	Baked Turkey Wings Smoky Greens	Turkey Sausage and Pepperoni Pizza Rolls
Monday	McDowell's Breakfast Burrito	Hot Chicken Salad Tomato Soup		
Tuesday		Tasty Turkey Chili Honey-Butter Corn Muffins		
Wednesday		Lasagna		
Thursday	Breakfast Muffins	Hot Chicken Salad		

Make sure you start with a clean kitchen. It can be stressful to attempt to cook when the pot or spatula you need is sitting underneath a pile of dirty dishes in the sink.

Gather everything you need to make a recipe before you start cooking. You learned about mise en place on page 15. Having everything in front of you saves a lot of time when cooking.

Clean as you go. Unless you have an unlimited supply of measuring spoons and other tools/equipment, you must wash dishes as you go along. If you need to coat any pans with nonstick spray, do so over the sink. Wipe down countertops as you finish each recipe also.

Prepare dishes in a specific order for maximum efficiency – prepare dishes that take a while to cook first. While the collard greens and lasagna cook you could prepare the smoothies, steamed zucchini and yellow squash, frittata, and tomato soup in the sample weekly menu.

Mise en place for Doritos-Crusted Chicken Tenders

Breakfast

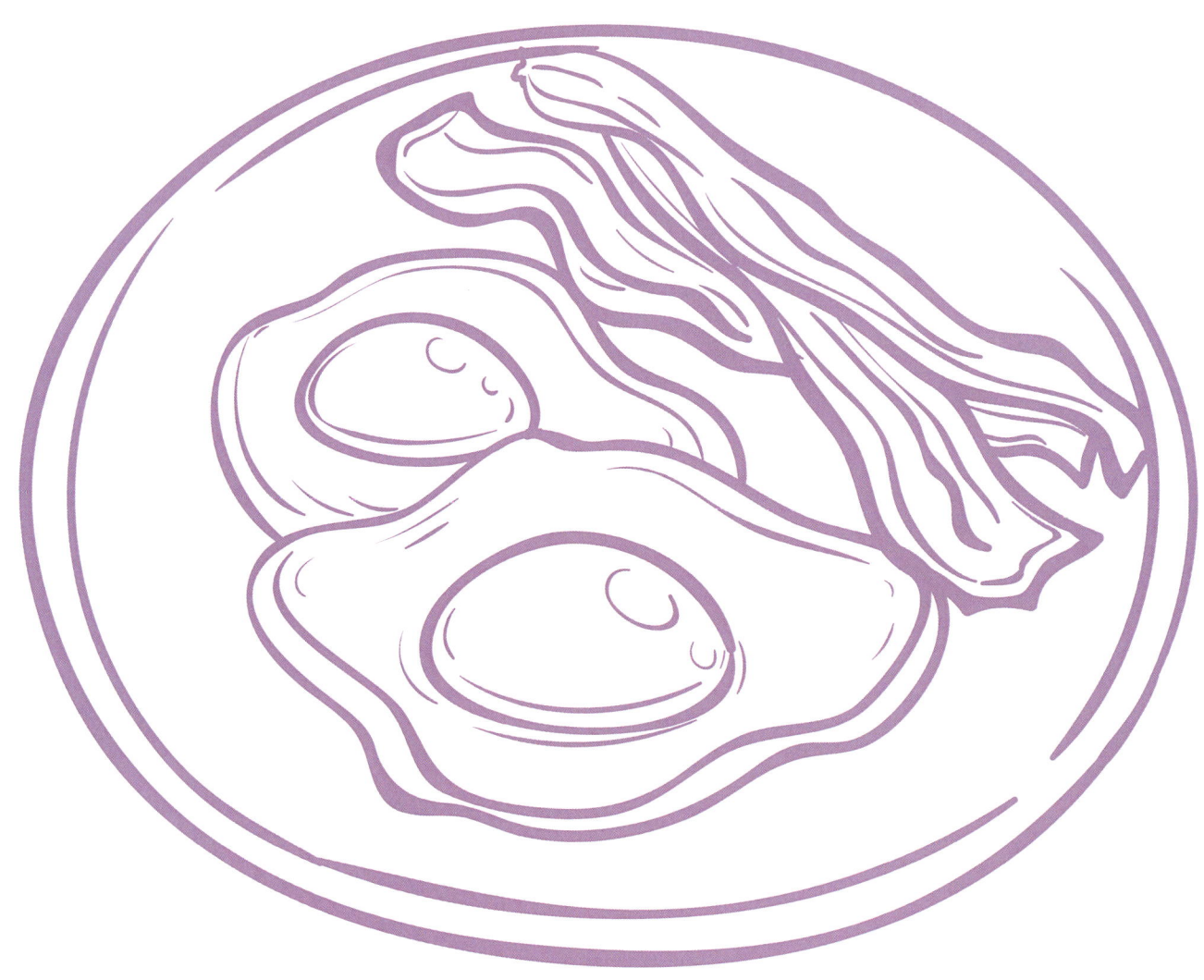

Frisky Frittata

 **Yield:** 4 servings   **Prep Time:** 10 minutes   **Total Time:** 30 minutes

Ingredients

- 8 large eggs
- ½ cup shredded Asiago cheese
- ½ tsp pepper
- 2 tsp extra-virgin olive oil
- 8 oz Italian chicken sausage, casings removed
- 8 oz baby bella mushrooms, sliced
- ½ cup diced red, yellow, purple or combination bell pepper
- ½ cup sliced yellow onion
- 2 cloves garlic, minced
- 1 tsp chopped fresh thyme or ½ tsp dried thyme
- 1 tsp chopped fresh rosemary or ½ tsp dried rosemary
- ½ tsp kosher salt
- ½ cup shredded mozzarella cheese

Directions

1. In a large bowl, whisk the eggs then whisk in the Asiago and pepper.
2. In a 10-inch nonstick skillet over medium-high heat, warm the olive oil. Add the sausage and cook until browned, about 5 minutes. Reduce the heat to medium and add the mushrooms, bell peppers, and onions; cook another 5 minutes. Stir in the garlic, thyme, rosemary, and salt. Reduce the heat to medium-low, add the eggs, and cover the pan. Cook undisturbed until the center begins to set, about 8 minutes.
3. Sprinkle the mozzarella over the top.
4. Place under the broiler for 2 minutes, until cheese is melted.

Mrs. Hopson's Breakfast Pie

My mother got this recipe from her hairdresser many years ago. It is one of the first recipes I learned to cook as a child. I make this often and enjoy it for breakfast, lunch, or dinner. I usually double the recipe and freeze one of the pies for later.

 **Yield:** 4 servings   **Prep Time:** 10 minutes   **Total Time:** 45 minutes

Ingredients

- 1 deep-dish pie crust
- 4 slices American cheese
- ½ lb Jennie-O All-Natural Turkey Sausage or Jimmy Dean Premium Pork Regular Sausage Roll
- ¼ cup diced yellow onion
- 4 large eggs
- ⅓ cup whole milk
- ½ cup grated mild cheddar cheese, plus more for topping
- ¼ teaspoon kosher salt
- Dash (⅛ tsp) pepper

Directions

1. Preheat the oven to 350°F.
2. Line the bottom of the pie crust with the sliced cheese.
3. Cook the sausage and onions in a medium-size skillet on medium heat until the sausage is browned and crumbled, about 6 minutes. Spread the sausage and onions on the bottom of the pie crust.
4. Beat the eggs with the milk, ½ cup grated cheese, salt, and pepper. Pour the egg mixture into the pie crust. Top with the additional grated cheese.
5. Bake for 25–30 minutes. Let cool for 5 minutes before slicing.

Mrs. Hopson's Breakfast Pie

Banana Pudding Smoothie

 **Yield:** 1 serving   **Prep Time:** 5 minutes   **Total Time:** 5 minutes

Ingredients

- *3 Medjool dates, pitted*
- *1 cup almond milk*
- *2 frozen peeled ripe bananas*
- *¼ cup old-fashioned rolled oats*
- *½ tsp vanilla extract*
- *½ tsp banana extract*
- *½ cup vanilla Greek yogurt*
- *3–4 vanilla wafers*

Directions

1. Place the dates and almond milk in a high-speed blender. Blend until smooth.
2. Add the remaining ingredients except wafers and blend until smooth and creamy.
3. Add wafers and pulse to combine, leaving chunks of wafers.

Strawberry Banana Smoothie, Banana Pudding Smoothie, Oreo Milkshake, Snickerdoodle Smoothie

Strawberry Banana Smoothie

 **Yield:** 1 serving   **Prep Time:** 5 minutes   **Total Time:** 5 minutes

Ingredients

- *1 cup almond milk*
- *1 large handful fresh baby spinach or kale (optional)*
- *1 frozen peeled banana*
- *1 cup frozen strawberries*
- *1 scoop vanilla protein powder*

Directions

1. Place the almond milk and greens in a high-speed blender and blend until the greens are liquified, about 60 seconds.
2. Stop the blender and add remaining ingredients.
3. Blend until smooth and creamy.

Breakfast Muffins

 **Yield:** 12 servings   **Prep Time:** 5 minutes   **Total Time:** 30 minutes

Ingredients

- 2 large eggs
- 3 cups cooked brown rice
- 1 cup cooked Italian chicken sausage
- 1 small sweet onion, diced
- ¼ cup chopped white mushrooms
- ½ cup grated Asiago or Parmesan cheese
- ⅓ cup whole milk
- ½ tsp kosher salt
- ½ tsp pepper
- ½ tsp dried oregano
- ½ tsp garlic powder

Directions

1. Preheat the oven to 350°F. Spray a 12-cup muffin pan with nonstick cooking spray.
2. Mix the eggs in a large bowl. Stir in the remaining ingredients.
3. Divide the mixture equally among the 12 muffin cups.
4. Bake for 20–25 minutes, until golden brown.

Country Sausage Egg Bites

 **Yield:** 12 servings   **Prep Time:** 10 minutes   **Total Time:** 25 minutes

Ingredients

- 6 turkey breakfast sausage patties from page 36, chopped, or 1 lb Jennie-O All-Natural Turkey Sausage or Jimmy Dean Premium Pork Regular Sausage Roll
- ½ tsp kosher salt, divided
- ½ cup diced yellow onion
- 6 large eggs
- ¼ cup cream cheese
- ¼ cup grated mozzarella or Gruyère cheese
- ¼ tsp pepper
- ½ tsp basil, dried or 1 Tbsp fresh basil

Directions

1. Preheat the oven to 350°F.
2. In a medium-size skillet over medium heat, cook the sausage, ¼ tsp of the salt, and the onion until the sausage is browned and crumbled; drain off the grease.
3. Combine the eggs, cream cheese, mozzarella, the remaining ¼ tsp salt, the pepper, and basil in a blender and blend to a uniform consistency.
4. Spray a mini-muffin pan with nonstick spray. Evenly distribute the chopped sausage among the muffin cups. Pour the egg mixture evenly over the sausage.
5. Bake for 13–15 minutes, until the top is cooked.

Country Sausage Egg Bites

Turkey Breakfast Sausage

Yield: 16 servings **Prep Time:** 5 minutes **Total Time:** 15 minutes (if cooking four or less at a time)

Ingredients

- 2 lb ground turkey
- ¼ cup quick-cooking oats
- 1 tsp onion powder
- 1 ½ tsp kosher salt
- 1 tsp pepper
- 1 tsp garlic powder
- 1 tsp dried sage
- ½ tsp dried rosemary
- 1 tsp dried thyme
- 2 tsp packed light brown sugar
- 1 tsp dried tarragon
- ½ tsp cayenne pepper or red pepper flakes

Directions

1. Combine all ingredients in a large bowl, mixing well with your hands.
2. Form mixture into 16 equal patties.
3. Heat a large nonstick skillet over medium-high heat. Place a few patties in the skillet at a time, making sure the pan is not too crowded. Cook on each side for 3–4 minutes, until there is no pink in the center of the patties.

Turkey Breakfast Sausage with Shape + Store Container

Mini Toaster Waffles

Yield: 4 to 8 servings (about 17 waffles)

Prep Time: 15 minutes

Total Time: 1 hour and 15 minutes

Ingredients

- 2 cups all-purpose flour
- ½ tsp kosher salt
- 3 Tbsp sugar
- 1 pinch nutmeg
- ½ tsp cinnamon
- 4 tsp baking powder
- 2 large eggs
- 1½ cups whole milk
- 2 tsp maple extract
- ⅓ cup vegetable oil
- 1 cup pecans, chopped (optional)

Directions

1. Preheat a mini waffle maker.
2. In a large bowl, combine the flour, salt, sugar, nutmeg, cinnamon, and baking powder.
3. Beat the eggs in a medium-size bowl. Add the milk, maple extract, and oil; stir to combine.
4. Slowly add the egg mixture to the flour mixture, stirring to combine. Stir in the pecans, if using.
5. Add 3 Tbsp of the waffle batter to your mini-waffle maker. Cook for 2–3 minutes, until golden brown. Continue with the remaining batter.

Note: *You will need a mini-waffle maker for this recipe; I recommend the Dash mini-waffle maker. You can make them in advance and place in the freezer. When you're ready to consume, just pop them in the toaster or microwave.*

Mini Toaster Waffles

Avocado Toast

Yield: 2 servings   **Prep Time:** 15 minutes   **Total Time:** 17 minutes

Ingredients

- 1 large avocado peeled, pitted, and mashed
- 1 Tbsp chopped red onion
- ½ tsp fresh lemon or lime juice
- ¼ tsp kosher salt
- Dash (1/8 tsp) pepper
- ¼ tsp minced garlic
- 1 tsp chopped fresh basil
- 1 small Roma tomato, chopped
- 2 slices sourdough bread, toasted
- 4 strips turkey bacon or bacon, cooked and chopped

Directions

1. In a small bowl, combine the mashed avocado, red onion, lemon or lime juice, salt, pepper, garlic, and basil. Fold in the chopped tomato.
2. Spread the avocado mixture equally on each piece of toast and sprinkle with bacon.

Note: If you don't have a toaster, you can place the bread in a 350°F oven for 5–8 minutes.

Snacks & Appetizers

Parmesan-Ranch Potato Chips

Yield: 2 servings   **Prep Time:** 30 minutes   **Total Time:** 55 minutes

Ingredients

- 2 russet potatoes, peeled
- 3 Tbsp grated Parmesan cheese
- 1 tsp garlic powder
- 1 Tbsp Hidden Valley Ranch seasoning
- 1 Tbsp dried rosemary
- ¼ tsp pepper
- Olive oil spray

Directions

1. Preheat the oven to 400°F.
2. Use a mandoline to slice the potatoes into ⅛-inch rounds, placing them in a large bowl filled with cold water to remove starch. Let them soak for 10 minutes.
3. Meanwhile, combine the Parmesan, garlic powder, ranch seasoning, rosemary, and pepper in a bowl.
4. Drain the potato water and fill the bowl with clean, cold water. Wait 10 more minutes.
5. Strain the potatoes and spread them on a paper towel lined–baking sheet. Pat dry with paper towels.
6. Remove the paper towels from the baking sheet. Adjust the chips again so they're all lying flat.
7. Spritz the chips with olive oil and sprinkle with the seasoning mixture. Flip the chips over, and repeat on the other side.
8. Bake the chips for 20–25 minutes, until golden brown.
9. Sprinkle the chips with any remaining seasoning mixture.

Air-Fryer Instructions

1. Preheat the air fryer to 375°F for 2 minutes. Put a pot of salted water on to boil.
2. Combine the Parmesan, garlic powder, ranch seasoning, rosemary, and pepper in a bowl.
3. Use a mandoline to slice the potatoes into ⅛-inch rounds.
4. Place the potatoes into the water and boil for 2 minutes.
5. Repeat steps 5 through 7 above, omitting the olive oil.
6. Spray the air fryer basket with olive oil, then put half of the potatoes into the air fryer.
7. Cook for a total of 15 minutes, opening the basket and shaking the potatoes after 7 minutes. Potato chips are done when they are light golden.
8. Remove chips from the basket, place in a bowl, and sprinkle with any remaining seasoning. Repeat with the remaining potatoes.

Thanksgiving Crescent Rolls

Yield: 8 servings (3 rolls each) **Prep Time:** 15 minutes **Total Time:** 30 minutes

Ingredients

- 1 Tbsp unsalted butter
- 1 Tbsp extra-virgin olive oil
- ½ cup chopped yellow onions
- ¼ cup chopped celery
- 1 lb ground turkey
- ½ tsp minced garlic
- 1 tsp kosher salt
- ½ tsp pepper
- ½ tsp dried sage
- 1 (8-oz) package cream cheese, cubed
- ¼ cup cornbread stuffing, crushed
- ⅓ cup dried cranberries
- 3 (8-oz) cans refrigerated crescent rolls
- 1 Tbsp unsalted butter, melted, for brushing (optional)

Directions

1. Preheat the oven to 375°F with a rack in the center position.
2. Melt the butter with the olive oil in a large skillet over medium heat. Add the onions and celery and sauté for 4 minutes.
3. Add the ground turkey, garlic, salt, pepper, and sage. Continue cooking another 4 minutes, breaking up the turkey with a spatula. Drain off the fat. Stir in the cream cheese, cornbread stuffing, and cranberries.
4. Unroll and separate the crescent rolls. Place a 1-tsp dollop of the cream cheese mixture in the center of the large end of each. Roll it toward the small end, enclosing the filling. Tuck the ends under and pinch the edges to ensure the filling is sealed in.
5. Arrange the rolls on an ungreased baking sheet. Bake for 11–15 minutes, until golden brown.
6. Brush the hot rolls with melted butter, if desired.

Notes: Make sure you keep the crescent rolls in the fridge until ready to use. If the dough gets too warm you will have difficulty working with it. Too many rolls to eat at one time? You can freeze baked rolls until needed. They will last in the freezer for two months. Want to bake the rolls as needed? You can freeze the filling, thaw, and prepare rolls as needed. The frozen filling will also last two months in the freezer.

Crab Dip

Yield: 6 to 8 servings   **Prep Time:** 5 minutes   **Total Time:** 35 minutes

Ingredients

- 1 (8-oz) package cream cheese, softened
- ¼ cup shredded Parmesan cheese
- ½ cup mayonnaise
- ½ cup plain Greek yogurt
- 1 Tbsp Dijon mustard
- 1 tsp Old Bay seasoning
- 1 Tbsp Worcestershire sauce
- 1 Tbsp chopped fresh tarragon
- Juice of half a lemon
- ½ tsp Tabasco sauce
- ½ tsp onion powder
- ½ tsp garlic powder
- ½ tsp paprika
- ½ tsp kosher salt
- ¼ tsp pepper
- 1 cup grated sharp cheddar cheese, divided
- 1 lb lump crabmeat
- Toasted bread or crackers, for serving

Directions

1. Preheat the oven to 350°F.
2. In a medium-size bowl combine the cream cheese, Parmesan, mayonnaise, yogurt, mustard, Old Bay, Worcestershire sauce, tarragon, lemon juice, Tabasco, onion powder, garlic powder, paprika, salt, pepper, and ¼ cup of the cheddar cheese; mix thoroughly. Fold in the crabmeat.
3. Spread the crabmeat mixture in an 8x8-inch baking dish or skillet. Sprinkle the remaining cheddar cheese over the top.
4. Bake for 25–30 minutes, until hot and bubbling.
5. Serve hot with toasted bread or crackers.

Crab Dip

Corn and Black Bean Relish

Yield: 4 to 6 servings **Prep Time:** 5 minutes **Total Time:** 5 minutes

Ingredients

- 1 (9.5-oz) bag Green Giant Simply Steam Street Corn Southwestern Style, drained
- ½ (15-oz) can black beans
- 2 tsp chopped cilantro
- 1 Tbsp fresh lime juice
- ¼ tsp cumin
- Kosher salt, to taste
- 1 tsp extra-virgin olive oil
- Tortilla chips, for serving (optional)

Directions

1. Prepare the frozen corn according to package directions. Let cool.
2. Stir the corn, beans, cilantro, lime juice, cumin, salt, and olive oil together in a bowl.
3. Store covered in the fridge until ready to use.
4. Enjoy with tortilla chips, if desired.

Turkey Pepperoni and Sausage Pizza Pockets

Who doesn't love a Hot Pocket? Kids can help with this easy recipe

Yield: 8 servings **Prep Time:** 15 minutes **Total Time:** 30 minutes

Ingredients

- 1 large egg
- 2 Tbsp water
- 1/8 tsp oregano
- ½ tsp dried parsley
- 1/8 tsp dried basil
- 1/8 tsp garlic powder
- 1/8 tsp onion powder
- 1/8 tsp kosher salt
- 1 package thin pizza crust, chilled
- All-purpose flour, for dusting
- 1 cup pizza sauce
- 1 (5-oz) package turkey pepperoni, chopped
- 4 ounces crumbled cooked turkey sausage
- 2 cups shredded mozzarella cheese

Directions

1. Preheat the oven to 400°F.
2. In a small bowl, combine the egg, water, herbs, and spices.
3. Unroll the crust onto a floured board. Using the bottom of the pie mold cut the crust into 16 rectangles.
4. Place one rectangle on the bottom of an open-face pie mold. Brush the edges with the egg wash. Spoon 1 teaspoon each of the pizza sauce, pepperoni, sausage, and mozzarella in the center.
5. Place another rectangle on the top of the pie filling. Close the pie mold to seal. Repeat with the remaining dough and fillings.
6. Place pies on a cookie sheet lined with a Silpat mat or parchment paper. Brush the egg wash on the tops of the pockets. Cut slits in the top of each pocket to allow steam to vent.
7. Bake for 15 minutes, until golden brown.

Note: *For this recipe you'll need a mini-pie mold and pastry brush. Don't have a pie mold? No problem! Follow these steps instead:*

1. Preheat the oven to 400°F.
2. In a small bowl, combine the egg, water, herbs, and spices.
3. Unroll the crust onto a floured board. The dough should measure about 16x14. Using a knife or pizza cutter, cut the crust into 8 rectangles.
4. Brush the edges with the egg wash. Spoon 1 teaspoon each of the pizza sauce, pepperoni, sausage, and mozzarella toward the edge of one short end being careful not to cover up the egg wash.
5. Fold the other short end on top of the filling making sure the dough edges are on top of each other. Seal the dough edges with a fork, forming a crimp design. Repeat with the remaining dough and fillings.
6. Place the pies on a cookie sheet lined with a Silpat mat or parchment paper. Brush the egg wash on the tops of the pockets. Cut slits in the top of each pocket to allow steam to vent.
7. Bake for 15 minutes, until golden brown.

Snickerdoodle Smoothie

Yield: 1 serving **Prep Time:** 5 minutes **Total Time:** 5 minutes

Ingredients

- ½ cup almond milk
- 3 Medjool dates, pitted
- 1 frozen peeled banana
- ¼ cup almond butter
- ½ tsp vanilla extract
- ¼ tsp cinnamon
- 1 pinch sea salt
- Ice (optional)

Directions

1. Place almond milk and dates in a high-speed blender. Blend until dates are completely liquified.
2. Add all remaining ingredients and blend until smooth and creamy.

Soups & Salads (& a Sandwich)

Chicken Noodle Soup

Scientific studies show that chicken noodle soup has anti-inflammatory properties and can help relieve cold and flu symptoms. But you don't really need an excuse to enjoy this wonderful soup any time of year. To save time, use store-bought rotisserie chicken.

Yield: 6 servings   **Prep Time:** 15 minutes   **Total Time:** 45 minutes

Ingredients

- 1 Tbsp unsalted butter
- 1 Tbsp extra-virgin olive oil
- 1 medium yellow onion, diced
- 2 stalks celery, diced
- 2 carrots, peeled and diced
- 1 tsp minced garlic
- 2 quarts water
- 2 cups diced or shredded cooked chicken
- 2 Tbsp plus 2 tsp L.B. Jamison's Chicken-Flavored Soup Base or Better Than Bouillon Roasted Chicken Base
- 2 tsp umami (mushroom) powder (optional)
- 3 cups uncooked wide egg noodles
- ½ tsp dried dill
- ½ tsp dried tarragon
- ½ tsp dried thyme
- 1 Tbsp dried parsley
- Kosher salt and pepper, to taste

Directions

1. In a large stockpot or Dutch oven, heat the butter and olive oil over medium-high heat. Add the onions, celery, and carrots (mirepoix) to the pot. Cook for 4 minutes, until the onions are translucent. Add the minced garlic. Cook for 1 minute.
2. Add the water to the pot; bring to a boil. Add the chicken, soup base, umami powder, and noodles. Cover, reduce the heat, and let simmer for about 10 minutes, until the noodles are tender.
3. Stir in the dill, tarragon, thyme, and parsley. Add salt and pepper as needed.

Chicken Tortilla Soup

Yield: 4 servings   **Prep Time:** 15 minutes   **Total Time:** 45 minutes

Ingredients

- 2 Tbsp extra-virgin olive oil
- 2 small red onions, finely chopped
- 1 stalk celery, finely chopped
- 4 tsp garlic paste
- 1 tsp kosher salt, divided
- 1 (10-oz) can Ro-Tel diced tomatoes and green chilies
- 1 cup low-sodium chicken broth
- 1 (10.5-oz) can condensed cream of chicken soup
- 2 tsp cumin
- 2 tsp chili powder
- ½ tsp dried cilantro
- Meat from 1 rotisserie chicken, shredded (about 2 ½ cups)
- 1 (15-oz) can seasoned black beans, drained
- 1 (15-oz) can cannellini beans, drained
- 1 (11-oz) can Green Giant Mexicorn
- 2 Tbsp fresh lime juice
- Tortilla strips
- 8 oz Monterey Jack cheese, grated

Directions

1. Heat the oil in a large pot over medium heat. Add the onions and celery. Sauté for 5–6 minutes, until softened and translucent.
2. Add the garlic paste and ½ tsp of the salt. Continue cooking for 1 minute.
3. Stir in the diced tomatoes, chicken broth, and soup. Add the remaining ½ tsp salt, the cumin, chili powder, and cilantro. Stir to combine. Add the chicken, beans, and Mexicorn. Simmer for 15–20 minutes, until heated through.
4. Stir in the lime juice.
5. Divide among four bowls and garnish each with tortilla strips and cheese.

Tasty Turkey Chili

I love to make this turkey chili with my Honey-Butter Corn Muffins (page 104) when it's cold outside. This recipe has a lot of ingredients, but it comes together quickly.

Yield: 6 servings   **Prep Time:** 10 minutes   **Total Time:** 45 minutes

Ingredients

- 2 Tbsp extra-virgin olive oil
- 2 lb ground turkey
- 1 cup chopped white onions
- 1 cup chopped celery (about 2 stalks)
- 1 cup chopped green pepper
- 1 (6-oz) can tomato paste
- 1 (10-oz) can Ro-Tel diced tomatoes
- 1 tsp garlic powder
- 3 Tbsp chili powder
- 1 tsp onion powder
- 2 tsp cumin
- 1 tsp seasoned salt
- ½ tsp pepper
- 1 tsp umami (mushroom) powder (optional)
- 1 Tbsp sugar
- 2 cups low-sodium chicken broth
- 2 Tbsp cornstarch
- 2 Tbsp cold water
- 1 (15-oz) can pinto beans, drained
- 1 (15-oz) can red kidney beans, drained

Directions

1. Heat the olive oil in a large pot over medium-high heat. Add the turkey and cook, stirring and breaking up the meat, for 6 minutes. Add the holy trinity (onions, celery, green pepper) and cook for an additional 3 minutes. Add the tomato paste, diced tomatoes, garlic powder, chili powder, onion powder, cumin, seasoned salt, pepper, umami powder, sugar, and broth. Bring to a boil. Reduce heat and simmer for 20 minutes.
2. Meanwhile, in a small bowl, combine the cornstarch and water to make a cornstarch slurry. Stir to combine.
3. Stir the beans into the chili.
4. Add the slurry to the pot and stir to combine. Cook another 5 minutes or so to allow the chili to thicken.

Cucumber Salad

Yield: 4 servings **Prep Time:** 5 minutes **Total Time:** 5 minutes (plus 1 hour and 20 minutes to sweat the cucumbers)

Ingredients

- 3 medium cucumbers, peeled, halved lengthwise, seeded, and sliced
- 1 tsp kosher salt
- ¾ cup sour cream
- 1 tsp Dijon mustard
- 1 ½ tsp balsamic vinegar
- 1 Tbsp finely chopped fresh dill or 1 tsp dried dill
- 1 pinch (⅛ tsp) sugar (optional)
- ¼ tsp pepper
- Half a medium red onion, sliced

Directions

1. Toss the cucumbers with the salt in a medium bowl. Let sit for 20 minutes. Transfer the cucumbers to a colander set over a bowl. Let sit for 1 hour. Drain the cucumbers and pat dry.
2. Whisk together the sour cream, mustard, vinegar, dill, sugar (if using), and pepper in a medium bowl.
3. Stir in the onions and cucumbers.
4. Store in the fridge until ready to serve.

Sweet Potato and Apple Bisque

Yield: 4 servings **Prep Time:** 10 minutes **Total Time:** 55 minutes

Ingredients

- 3 Tbsp extra-virgin olive oil
- 3 medium sweet potatoes, diced large
- 2 Granny Smith apples, diced large
- 1 Tbsp chopped fresh sage or 1 tsp dried sage
- ¼ tsp grated fresh nutmeg
- ¼ tsp cinnamon
- 1 small red onion, chopped
- 2 cups low-sodium chicken broth
- 1 cup heavy cream
- Kosher salt and pepper, to taste

Directions

1. Warm the olive oil in a soup pot over medium-high heat. Add the sweet potatoes and cook until they're fork-tender.
2. Add the apples, sage, nutmeg, cinnamon, and onions. Cook until the apples are tender and the onions are translucent. Add the chicken broth. Simmer for 10–15 minutes. Let cool for 10 minutes.
3. Pour the soup into a high-speed blender or food processor and purée until smooth.
4. Return the soup to the pot over medium low heat and warm through. Stir in the cream and add salt and pepper to taste.

Sweet Potato and
Apple Bisque

Tomato Soup

Yield: 4 servings **Prep Time:** 5 minutes **Total Time:** 35 minutes

Ingredients

- 2 Tbsp extra-virgin olive oil
- 2 Tbsp unsalted butter
- 1 large yellow onion, sliced thin
- ½ tsp kosher salt
- ¼ tsp pepper
- 1 Tbsp minced garlic
- 1 Tbsp tomato paste
- 1 (28-oz) can peeled San Marzano tomatoes
- 3 cups water, low-sodium vegetable stock, or chicken stock/broth
- 1 pinch (⅛ tsp) sugar
- 1 cup chopped basil, plus more for garnish
- Leaves from 2 sprigs fresh thyme or ½ tsp dried thyme

Directions

1. Heat the olive oil and butter in a large saucepan over medium heat. Add the onions to the pan with the salt and pepper. Cook for 5 minutes. Add the minced garlic and tomato paste. Cook for 2 minutes. Add the tomatoes, water or stock/broth, and sugar; bring to a boil. Reduce the heat and simmer for 10–15 minutes.
2. Transfer the soup, thyme, and basil to a blender to purée. You may need to work in batches depending on the size of your blender.
3. Return the soup to the pot and heat through. Adjust the seasoning, if needed, and serve with a sprinkle of chopped basil.

Note: Tomatoes react with cast iron saucepans, so to avoid bitter- or metallic-tasting soup, use a stainless steel or nonstick saucepan.

Grilled Cheese Sandwich and Tomato Soup

Grilled Cheese Sandwich

Yield: 2 servings **Prep Time:** 5 minutes **Total Time:** 20 minutes

Ingredients

- ¼ cup (4 Tbsp) unsalted butter, softened
- 1 tsp Dijon mustard
- ⅛ tsp garlic powder
- ⅛ tsp onion powder
- ½ tsp kosher salt
- 1 tsp dried oregano
- 4 slices bread
- ½ cup shredded cheddar or mozzarella cheese, divided

Directions

1. Preheat a skillet over medium heat.
2. In a small bowl mix, the butter, mustard, garlic powder, onion powder, salt, and oregano together.
3. Generously butter one side of two slices of bread. Place both butter-side-down in the skillet and top each evenly with ¼ cup cheese.
4. Butter the two remaining slices of bread on one side and place both butter-side-up on top of sandwiches. Grill until lightly browned and flip over; continue grilling until cheese is melted.

*Savory Broccoli Salad,
Avocado Ranch Dressing,
Cucumber Salad*

Savory Broccoli Salad

Yield: 4 servings **Prep Time:** 15 minutes **Total Time:** 15 minutes

Ingredients

- 5 strips turkey bacon
- 4 cups fresh broccoli florets (about ½ lb)
- 1 tsp chopped fresh tarragon or ½ tsp dried tarragon
- ½ cup dried sweetened cranberries
- ½ tsp minced garlic
- ¼ cup Avocado Ranch dressing (page 61)

Directions

1. Place the bacon in a cold, medium size skillet. Place the pan over medium high heat and cook the bacon until crispy on both sides. Drain on paper towels, if necessary, then crumble the bacon.
2. Cook the broccoli in boiling water for 2–3 minutes. Strain and place in a bowl of cold water.
3. Combine the bacon, broccoli, tarragon, cranberries, and garlic in a large bowl. Toss with Avocado Ranch Dressing to coat.

Avocado Ranch Dressing

Yield: 8 servings **Prep Time:** 5 minutes **Total Time:** 5 minutes

Ingredients

- 1 large ripe avocado
- ½ tsp Dijon mustard
- 1 Tbsp Hidden Valley Ranch dressing mix
- ½ cup mayonnaise
- 1 cup buttermilk

Directions

1. Combine all ingredients in a food processor except buttermilk. With the food processor blender on high, slowly add buttermilk from the top, blending until desired consistency.

Note: If you don't have a food processor you can use a blender.

Apple Pecan Chicken Salad

Yield: 4 servings   **Prep Time:** 10 minutes   **Total Time:** 10 minutes

Ingredients

- *2 cups mixed baby greens*
- *2 cups chopped romaine lettuce*
- *½ cup chopped pecans*
- *¼ cup blue cheese crumbles*
- *1 cup diced cooked chicken*
- *Half a Red Delicious apple, cut into wedges*
- *Half a Granny Smith apple, cut into wedges*
- *½ cup store-bought dressing, such as Hidden Valley Original Ranch Topping and Dressing*

Directions

1. Combine all ingredients in a large bowl and toss well.
2. Divide the salad among four plates; serve immediately.

Apple and Cabbage Slaw

Yield: 4 servings **Prep Time:** 10 minutes **Total Time:** 10 minutes

Ingredients

- 1 small head of cabbage, cored and finely shredded or 1 bag shredded cabbage
- Half a sweet onion, sliced
- 1 Granny Smith apple, julienned or cut into strips
- ½ cup mayonnaise or plain Greek yogurt
- 1 Tbsp Dijon mustard
- 2 Tbsp apple cider vinegar
- 1 Tbsp sugar
- Kosher salt and pepper, to taste

Directions

1. In a large bowl, combine the cabbage, onions, and apples.
2. Whisk the mayo, mustard, vinegar, and sugar together.
3. Pour the dressing mix into the slaw and toss to coat.
4. Add salt and pepper to taste.

Southwest Chicken Salad

Yield: 4 to 6 servings   **Prep Time:** 10 minutes   **Total Time:** 12 minutes

Ingredients

- 4 cups chopped romaine lettuce
- 4 cups chopped iceberg lettuce
- ¾ cup shredded red cabbage
- ¾ cup shredded carrots
- ¾ cup Kraft Mexican shredded cheese or shredded Monterey Jack cheese
- 1 cup corn and black bean relish (see page 46)
- ¾ cup store-bought spicy dressing, such as Hidden Valley Southwest Chipotle Topping & Dressing, or to taste
- 16 oz grilled chicken breast strips
- ½ cup grape tomatoes
- 1 cup Fresh Gourmet Santa Fe–style tortilla strips

Directions

1. Combine the lettuces, cabbage, carrots, cheese, and relish in a large bowl. Add two-thirds of the dressing and toss to coat. Add remaining dressing, if necessary.
2. Divide the salad among serving plates. Top with chicken, tomatoes, and tortilla strips.

Southwest Chicken Salad and Apple Pecan Chicken Salad

Chicken Salad in Tomato Shells

This recipe was inspired by a posting on a cooking channel website. It was tweaked to reduce the amount of sodium, as well as to use my favorite mustard (although any mustard will suffice) and rotisserie chicken—a grocery store shortcut. I prefer lemon-pepper rotisserie chicken, but any flavor could be used. I also like the extra crunch and nutty flavor of the pecans.

Yield: 4 servings **Prep Time:** 30 minutes **Total Time:** 30 minutes

Ingredients

- ½ cup chopped pecans (optional)
- Meat from 1 rotisserie chicken, diced (4 cups)
- ¼ cup chopped Vidalia or other sweet onion
- 1 stalk celery, diced
- 1 tsp chopped fresh tarragon or ½ tsp dried tarragon
- 1 tsp chopped fresh dill or ½ tsp dried dill
- 1 Tbsp chopped fresh parsley or ½ Tbsp dried parsley
- ½ cup mayonnaise
- 2 tsp fresh lemon juice
- 1 tsp Pommery stone-ground mustard
- ½ tsp kosher salt
- ¼ tsp pepper
- Baked Tomato Shells (next page)

Directions

1. If using pecans, toast them in a skillet over medium heat or roast at 350°F for 10 minutes.
2. Place the chicken, onion, celery, tarragon, dill, and parsley in a large bowl.
3. Mix the mayo, lemon juice, mustard, salt, and pepper in a small bowl.
4. Toss the mayo mixture with the chicken. Add the pecans, if using.
5. Fill each tomato shell with the chicken salad.

Continued on page 68

Chicken Salad in Tomato Shells

Baked Tomato Shells

Yield: 4 servings   **Prep Time:** 5 minutes   **Total Time:** 20 minutes

Continued from page 66

Ingredients

- 2 large tomatoes, cut in half horizontally
- 2 tsp extra-virgin olive oil, divided
- 1 tsp chopped fresh basil or ½ tsp dried basil
- Kosher salt and pepper, to taste

Directions

1. Preheat the oven to 350°F.
2. Scoop out all the pulp and seeds from each tomato half and set tomatoes on a baking sheet.
3. Put ½ tsp olive oil in each half, using your fingers to spread it around the insides to coat.
4. Sprinkle the basil, salt, and pepper in each half. Bake for 15 minutes. Let cool.

Poultry

Doritos-Crusted Chicken Tenders

Yield: 4 servings **Prep Time:** 15 minutes **Total Time:** 30 minutes

Ingredients

- 1 cup all-purpose flour
- ½ tsp kosher salt
- ¼ tsp pepper
- 2 large eggs
- 2 Tbsp whole milk or water
- 1 (14.5 oz) bag Nacho Cheese Doritos
- 4 skinless boneless chicken breasts, cut into 2-inch strips
- Southwestern Dipping Sauce, for serving (see page 72)

Directions

1. Preheat the oven to 400°F.
2. Combine the flour, salt, and pepper in a shallow bowl.
3. Mix the eggs and milk or water in another shallow bowl.
4. Pulse the Doritos in a food processor until they resemble a cross between bread crumbs and cornflakes. Place the Doritos in a third shallow bowl.
5. Place each chicken strip in the flour and toss to coat, then dip it into the egg mixture, then roll it in the Doritos. Place them on a nonstick baking sheet as you go.
6. Bake in the oven for 15 minutes, until golden brown, turning halfway through.
7. Serve hot with Southwestern Dipping Sauce.

Doritos-Crusted Chicken Tenders and Southwestern Dipping Sauce

Southwestern Dipping Sauce

Yield: 6 servings **Prep Time:** 5 minutes **Total Time:** 5 minutes

Ingredients

- ½ cup mayonnaise
- 1 tsp fresh lemon juice
- 1 tsp hot sauce
- Pinch (1/8 tsp) of crushed Doritos
- Pinch (1/8 tsp) of kosher salt
- Pinch (1/8 tsp) of paprika

Directions

1. Add all ingredients in a small bowl and stir to combine.
2. Cover and chill in the fridge until ready to use.

Hot Chicken Salad

Yield: 8 servings **Prep Time:** 15 minutes **Total Time:** 40 minutes

Ingredients

- 2 cups cubed cooked chicken
- ½ tsp kosher salt
- ½ tsp pepper
- 2 Tbsp fresh lemon juice
- ¼ tsp garlic powder
- 1 cup chopped celery
- ½ cup shredded mozzarella cheese
- 4 oz cream cheese
- 1 (10.75-oz) can condensed cream of mushroom soup
- ½ cup sour cream
- ¼ tsp onion powder
- ½ cup slivered almonds
- 1 cup crushed potato chips

Directions

1. Preheat the oven to 350°F. Grease an 8x8-inch baking dish or spray it with cooking spray.
2. Combine all the ingredients except the potato chips in a large mixing bowl.
3. Pour the mixture into the baking dish. Top with the potato chips.
4. Bake for 20–25 minutes, until bubbling.

Chicken Pot Pie

Yield: 6 to 8 servings **Prep Time:** 15 minutes **Total Time:** 50 minutes

Ingredients

- 1 ½ cups low-sodium chicken broth
- 1 tsp Better Than Bouillon Roasted Chicken soup base
- 2 Tbsp extra-virgin olive oil
- 1 cup frozen pearl onions
- 1 cup frozen peas and carrots
- 3 stalks celery, diced
- 1 tsp minced garlic
- 1 (10.5-oz) can condensed cream of chicken soup
- ¼ cup white wine (optional)
- ½ tsp kosher salt, or to taste
- ½ tsp pepper, or to taste
- 1 tsp dried dill or 1½ Tbsp minced fresh dill
- 1 tsp dried rosemary or 2 tsp minced fresh rosemary
- 1 Tbsp cornstarch
- 2 Tbsp cold water, divided
- 5 ½ cups large-diced cooked chicken breast
- 2 deep dish-pie crust, thawed
- 1 refrigerated pie crust sheet
- 1 large egg

Directions

1. Preheat the oven to 400°F.
2. In a small saucepan bring the chicken broth and Better Than Bouillon to a boil, stirring to incorporate. Remove from heat.
3. Heat the olive oil in a large Dutch oven over medium heat. Add the onions, peas and carrots, and celery and sauté about 4 minutes, until onions are translucent. Add the garlic and cook for 1 minute. Add the cream of chicken soup, wine (if using), hot chicken broth, salt, pepper, dill, and rosemary.
4. Mix the cornstarch and 1 Tbsp of the water in a cup until smooth. Add to the pot and stir it in.
5. Let simmer for 5 minutes, stirring, until the sauce is thickened. Taste and add more salt or pepper, if needed.
6. Add the chicken to the pot and mix well.
7. Pour the filling into the deep-dish pie crust. Unfold the pie crust sheet and place it over the filling. Use a knife to trim any excess dough around the edges. Use your fingers or a fork to crimp the edges together.
8. Mix the egg with 1 Tbsp water in a small bowl to make an egg wash.
9. Brush the egg wash over the top of the crust. Cut three slits in the top of the crust. Bake for 35 minutes, until the crust is golden brown.

Note: To freeze, place the uncooked pie in an airtight container and store in the freezer. Thaw the pie in the refrigerator the night before you want to serve it. Bake in a 400°F oven for 35 minutes, until the crust is golden brown.

Chicken Pot Pie

Baked Turkey Wings

Yield: 4 servings   **Prep Time:** 20 minutes   **Total Time:** 2 hours and 20 minutes

Ingredients

- 1 large yellow onion, chopped
- 1 small green bell pepper, chopped
- 1 small red bell pepper, chopped
- ½ tsp minced garlic
- 1 tsp poultry seasoning, divided
- ½ tsp kosher salt
- ¼ tsp pepper
- 1 cup low-sodium chicken broth
- 4 turkey wings, rinsed and patted dry
- ½ tsp umami (mushroom) powder (optional)
- ½ tsp dried sage
- ½ tsp dried thyme
- ½ tsp seasoned salt
- 1 packet Lipton onion soup mix
- 1 (10.75-oz) can condensed cream of mushroom soup
- ½ cup water
- 4 cups cooked rice, for serving

Directions

1. Preheat the oven to 350°F.
2. Place the onion and bell peppers in the bottom of a 13x9-inch baking dish. Sprinkle the garlic, ½ tsp of the poultry seasoning, salt, and pepper on the onion and peppers. Stir to evenly distribute. Pour the chicken broth in the side of the pan so as not to disturb the vegetables. Place the turkey wings on top.
3. Mix the remaining ½ tsp poultry seasoning, the umami powder, sage, thyme, and seasoned salt together in small bowl. Sprinkle the mixture over the wings. Sprinkle the onion soup mix on top of the wings.
4. Cover the pan tightly with aluminum foil. Bake for 1 hour, until browned.
5. Stir the cream of mushroom soup and water together in a bowl.
6. Remove the wings from the oven. Pour the soup over the wings. Cover tightly and bake for 45 minutes. Remove the foil and bake 15 minutes more, until browned and bubbling. Wings are done when they reach an internal temp of 165°F.
7. Serve over hot rice.

Baked Turkey Wings

Amazing Italian Stuffed Peppers

Stuffed peppers are a fairly quick and easy meal to get into the oven if you have cooked rice on hand. I love to use different colors because they are pretty and cheerful. Please note that they vary in sweetness based on their color: Red is the sweetest, followed by yellow, then orange. Green peppers are the least sweet because they stay on the vine for the least amount of time, so they don't have time to develop the natural sugars other peppers get or a chance to change color.

Yield: 4 servings
Prep Time: 10 minutes
Total Time: 1 hour and 15 minutes

Ingredients

- 4 large bell peppers (any color)
- 1 Tbsp extra-virgin olive oil
- 1 lb Italian chicken sausage, casings removed
- ½ cup diced yellow onion
- 1 clove garlic, minced
- 1 tsp kosher salt
- ½ tsp pepper
- 1 tsp chopped fresh basil or ½ tsp dried basil
- 1 tsp chopped fresh oregano or ½ tsp dried oregano
- 1 cup cooked brown rice
- ¼ cup grated Parmesan cheese
- 1 cup grated mozzarella cheese, divided

Directions

1. Preheat the oven to 350°F.
2. Cut the top off each bell pepper and remove the core and seeds; rinse peppers.
3. Warm the olive oil in a skillet over medium heat. Add the sausage and onion. Cook for about 5 minutes, breaking up the sausage. Add the garlic, salt, pepper, basil, and oregano. Cook for another 3 minutes. Stir in the brown rice and Parmesan. Cook until heated through; remove from heat.
4. Pour a small amount of water in the bottom of an 8x8-inch baking dish.
5. Stir ½ cup of the mozzarella into the rice mixture. Fill the peppers with the rice mixture.
6. Place the peppers in the baking dish and cover with aluminum foil.
7. Bake for 30 minutes. Remove foil. Add the remaining mozzarella cheese to the tops of each pepper. Bake another 15 minutes longer, until peppers are tender.

Amazing Italian Stuffed Peppers

Chicken Parmesan

This recipe was inspired by a little-known, short-lived offering from a popular fast-food chain. Rather than prepare a sauce for the noodles, I decided to use a blast from the past: ramen noodles.

Note the difference between shredded and grated Parmesan cheese: Shredded Parmesan cheese consists of long, thin strips while grated Parmesan cheese looks very similar to powder. The two are not interchangeable and often appear in the same recipe.

Yield: 4 servings
Prep Time: 15 minutes
Total Time: 40 minutes

Ingredients

- 1 large egg
- ½ cup shredded Parmesan cheese
- ¼ cup grated Parmesan cheese
- ½ tsp kosher salt
- ¼ tsp dried tarragon
- ¼ tsp dried thyme
- ¼ tsp dried rosemary
- ¼ tsp garlic powder
- ¼ tsp onion powder
- 1 Tbsp powdered sugar
- ¼ cup cornstarch
- ¼ cup dry Italian bread crumbs
- 4 boneless, skinless chicken breasts
- ½ cup jarred marinara sauce or leftover marinara sauce from Lasagna (page 142)
- ½ cup shredded mozzarella cheese
- 2 packages Maruchan Creamy Chicken ramen noodles
- 1 cup grape tomatoes, cut in half
- 1 cup chopped spinach
- 1 lemon, cut in half

Directions

1. Preheat the oven to 375°F.
2. Place the egg in a shallow pan and beat it with a fork.
3. In another shallow pan combine the Parmesan cheeses, the salt, tarragon, thyme, rosemary, garlic powder, onion powder, powdered sugar, cornstarch, and bread crumbs.
4. Dip each chicken breast in the beaten egg, then place in the dish with the Parmesan cheese mixture and flip to coat. Place each chicken breast on a baking sheet.
5. Bake for 30 minutes. Take chicken out of the oven and spread 2 tablespoons marinara sauce on each breast. Sprinkle with 2 tablespoons of the mozzarella each. Bake another 5–10 minutes.
6. Prepare the ramen noodles according to package directions. Strain the noodles. Add the tomatoes and spinach to the pan with the noodles. Cover and cook for 4 minutes, until spinach starts to wilt.
7. Squeeze lemon juice over the noodles.
8. Place a chicken breast on each of four plates. Divide the pasta equally among the plates next to the chicken.

Chicken Parmesan

Baked Chicken Breasts

This recipe can be used in any recipe that calls for cooked chicken. It is always a good idea to keep cooked chicken on hand for salads and soups. If you don't want to buy pickle juice, you can use a more traditional salt-water brine. You will need to start prepping for this recipe the night before.

Yield: 4 servings
Prep Time: 10 minutes
Total Time: 40 minutes (plus 8 hours to brine the chicken)

Ingredients

- 4 (6-oz) boneless, skinless chicken breasts
- 2 cups pickle juice or 2 Tbsp kosher salt dissolved in 2 cups water
- ½ tsp kosher salt
- ¼ tsp pepper
- ½ tsp onion powder
- ½ tsp garlic powder
- ¾ tsp smoked paprika
- ½ tsp dried rosemary
- 1 Tbsp extra-virgin olive oil

Directions

1. Place the chicken and brine (pickle juice) in a container with a lid, making sure there is enough brine to completely cover the chicken. Chill the container in the fridge for 6–8 hours.
2. Preheat the oven to 350°F.
3. In a small bowl, combine the salt, pepper, onion powder, garlic powder, smoked paprika, and rosemary.
4. Remove the chicken from the brine and rinse with cold water. Pat dry with paper towels.
5. Coat the chicken with the olive oil. Sprinkle the spice mixture on both sides of the chicken.
6. Place the chicken in a 9x13-in baking dish lined with aluminum foil. Bake for 30 minutes or until a meat thermometer inserted into the chicken registers 165°F.

Notes: You don't have to wait until all your dill pickles are gone to use pickle juice. You can purchase pickle juice separately from the grocery store or online (see Resources section on page 162). Pickle juice can also be consumed to help with muscle cramps; measure 2–3 oz and drink as a shot.

If you'd prefer a salt-water brine, add ¾ cup of kosher salt to 1 gallon warm water and stir to dissolve the salt. Let cool before using.

Baked Chicken Thighs with Balsamic Glaze

Yield: 4 servings
Prep Time: 10 minutes
Total Time: 45 minutes (plus 8 hours to brine the chicken)

Ingredients

- 1 gallon warm water
- ¾ cup kosher salt, plus more to taste
- 2 lb boneless skinless chicken thighs
- 2 Tbsp unsalted butter
- 4 Tbsp extra-virgin olive oil, divided
- 1 yellow onion, sliced
- Pepper, to taste
- 1 cup low-sodium chicken broth
- 1 Tbsp Dijon mustard
- 2 packets Lipton onion soup mix
- ½ tsp dried tarragon
- ½ tsp dried rosemary
- ¼ cup balsamic vinegar
- ¼ cup packed light brown sugar
- 3 tsp garlic paste
- ¼ tsp seasoned salt
- 1 Tbsp soy sauce

Directions

1. Place the water and salt in a container with a lid; allow the water to cool; add the chicken; make sure there is enough liquid to completely cover the chicken. Place the container in the fridge to marinate for 8–12 hours.
2. Preheat the oven to 350°F. Line the bottom of a 9x13-in baking dish with aluminum foil.
3. Remove the chicken from the brine and pat dry with paper towels.
4. Heat 2 Tbsp butter and 2 Tbsp of the olive oil in a large skillet over high heat. Sauté the onions until soft.
5. Place the onions in the bottom of the prepared baking dish. Place the chicken thighs on top of the onions. Sprinkle with salt and pepper.
6. In a large bowl, whisk together the chicken broth, remaining 2 Tbsp olive oil, mustard, onion soup mix, tarragon, rosemary, balsamic vinegar, brown sugar, garlic paste, seasoned salt, and soy sauce. Add salt and pepper to taste. Pour sauce over chicken.
7. Top the baking dish with aluminum foil. Bake for 30 minutes or until a meat thermometer inserted into the chicken registers 160°F. Chicken is safe to eat when it gets to 165°F but it will continue to cook to that temperature once it is out of the oven (this is known as carry-over cooking).
8. Let chicken rest 5 minutes before cutting.

Air-Fried Lemon Pepper Chicken Wings

Yield: 2-4 servings **Prep Time:** 10 minutes **Total Time:** 45 minutes

Ingredients

- 2 lb chicken wings
- ½ tsp smoked paprika
- ½ tsp kosher salt
- ¼ tsp pepper
- 1½ Tbsp cornstarch
- 1 tsp plus 2 Tbsp lemon pepper seasoning, divided
- ¼ cup (4 Tbsp) unsalted butter, melted
- ¼ tsp garlic paste

Directions

1. Preheat the air fryer to 400°F.
2. Rinse the chicken wings under running water in the sink. Pat them dry with a paper towel and place them in a large bowl.
3. In a small bowl, combine the smoked paprika, salt, and pepper.
4. Sprinkle the paprika mixture over the chicken and toss to coat well.
5. In a bowl, combine the cornstarch and 1 tsp of the lemon pepper seasoning.
6. Dip each wing into the cornstarch mixture and toss to coat well.
7. Place the wings in a single layer in the air fryer. Depending on the size of your air fryer, you will need to cook them in at least two batches. Bake for 20 minutes, flipping the wings halfway through. Place the cooked wings on a rack while the remaining batches are cooking.
8. In a small bowl, combine the melted butter, the remaining 2 Tbsp lemon pepper seasoning, and the garlic paste.
9. Brush the wings with the butter.
10. Place all the wings back into the air fryer to cook for another 3 minutes.

Note: There is a debate regarding cleaning chicken prior to cooking. Chicken contains pathogens like salmonella that even chefs like Julia Child prefer to remove before cooking. Other chefs, as well as the Center for Disease Control, recommend skipping this step and letting the cooking process kill bacteria. If you decide to clean your chicken, make sure you sanitize the sink, counter, cutting boards, and any other tools used around the kitchen afterwards.

Seafood

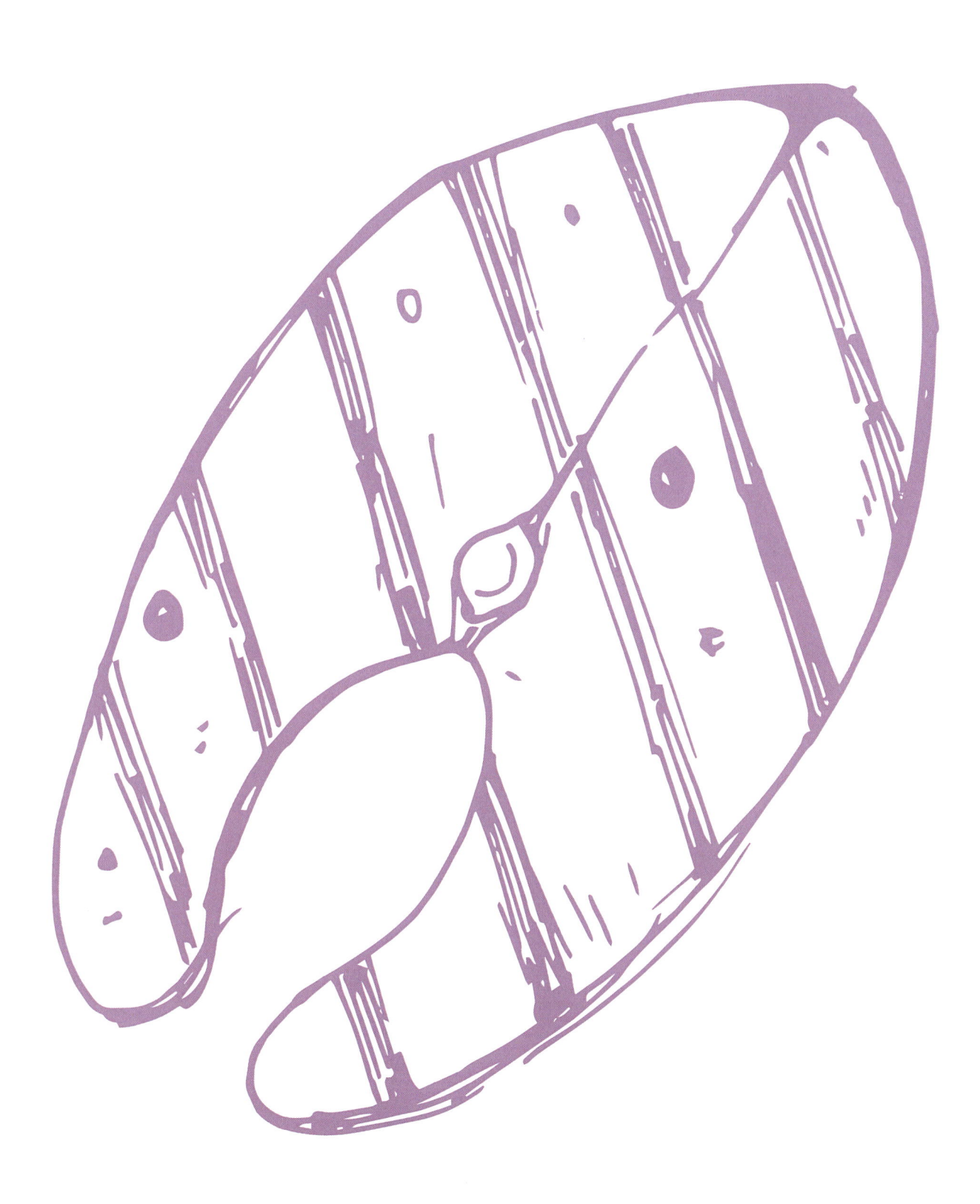

Tuna Salad

Yield: 4 servings **Prep Time:** 5 minutes **Total Time:** 15 minutes

Ingredients

- 2 (5–6-oz) cans tuna packed in water, drained
- 2 hard-boiled eggs, chopped
- 1 stalk celery, chopped
- ¼ cup mayonnaise
- ½ Tbsp Dijon mustard
- 1 Tbsp sweet pickle relish or dill relish
- Kosher salt and pepper, to taste
- Crackers, for serving

Directions

Combine the tuna, eggs, celery, mayo, mustard, relish, and salt and pepper in a medium-size bowl. Serve chilled with crackers.

Seafood Pot Pie

Yield: 4 servings **Prep Time:** 10 minutes **Total Time:** 50 minutes

Ingredients

- 1 (10.5-oz) can condensed cream of celery soup
- 1 (10.5-oz) can condensed cream of shrimp soup
- 1½ tsp Better Than Bouillon lobster base
- 1 tsp fresh lemon juice
- 1 tsp dried basil
- 2 tsp Old Bay seasoning, divided
- ½ tsp pepper
- ½ tsp onion powder
- ½ cup heavy cream
- Kosher salt, to taste
- 2 Tbsp unsalted butter
- ½ lb peeled and deveined raw shrimp
- ½ lb scallops, chopped
- 1½ tsp lemon pepper
- 8 oz real lump or imitation crabmeat
- 1 (6.5-oz) can chopped clams, drained
- 1 (10-oz) package frozen mixed vegetables (carrots, green beans, corn, peas), thawed
- 1 (13.2-oz) package Jus-Roll Puff Pastry, no thawing required

Directions

1. Preheat the oven to 375°F. Spray a 2-quart square baking dish with nonstick cooking spray.
2. In a bowl, combine the soups, lemon juice, basil, ½ tsp Old Bay seasoning, lobster base, pepper, onion powder, and heavy cream. Mix well. Add salt to taste, if needed.
3. Melt the butter in a large skillet over medium heat.
4. In a large bowl, combine the shrimp, scallops, lemon pepper and remaining 1½ tsp Old Bay seasoning.
5. Place the shrimp and scallops in the skillet and cook for 2 minutes.
6. Add the shrimp, scallops, crabmeat, clams, and mixed vegetables to the bowl and mix well.
7. Pour mixture into baking dish. Unroll the puff pastry, and lay it out on top of the filling.
8. Bake for 40 minutes, until bubbling and the crust is golden brown. Let cool for 5 minutes before serving.

Air-Fried Salmon Patties

Yield: 2 servings   **Prep Time:** 30 minutes   **Total Time:** 35 minutes

Ingredients

- 1 (14.75-oz) can salmon, drained
- ½ cup fresh bread crumbs
- ½ teaspoon onion powder
- 1 teaspoon Dijon mustard
- 1 large egg
- 1 teaspoon fresh lemon juice
- ½ teaspoon minced garlic
- ¼ teaspoon kosher salt
- ⅛ teaspoon pepper
- 1 tablespoon chopped fresh parsley or 1 teaspoon dried parsley
- 1 tablespoon chopped fresh dill or 1 teaspoon dried dill
- Olive oil cooking spray

Directions

1. In a large bowl, combine the salmon, bread crumbs, onion powder, mustard, egg, lemon juice, garlic, salt, pepper, parsley, and dill.
2. Form the mixture into 8 equal patties.
3. Spray the bottom of the air fryer basket with olive oil or cooking spray.
4. Preheat the air fryer to 400°F for 3 minutes.
5. Place the patties into the air fryer basket. Spray the tops of the patties with olive oil.
6. Cook for 8 minutes on each side.

Note: Check the canned salmon to ensure there are no skin and bones included. If there are, remove them, unless you like eating bones (some people do).

Air-Fried Salmon Patties

Tuna Pasta

Yield: 4 servings   **Prep Time:** 5 minutes   **Total Time:** 25 minutes

Ingredients

- 8 oz dried spaghetti
- 1 Tbsp plus ½ tsp kosher salt, divided
- 2 Tbsp extra-virgin olive oil
- 1 tsp minced garlic
- 2 (5-oz) cans tuna packed in olive oil, drained
- 1 (10.5-oz) can condensed cream of mushroom soup
- ¼ cup basil pesto
- 1 tsp Dijon mustard (optional)
- ¼ tsp pepper
- ⅓ cup shredded Parmesan cheese

Directions

1. Bring a large pot of water to a boil. Add 1 Tbsp salt, and cook the spaghetti according to the package directions. Strain.
2. Meanwhile, heat the olive oil in a large skillet over medium-high heat. Add the garlic to the skillet and cook for 1 minute. Reduce heat to medium. Add the tuna, soup, pesto, mustard, the remaining ½ tsp salt, and pepper to the skillet. Heat through.
3. Add the noodles to the skillet. Stir to coat.
4. Divide the pasta evenly among four bowls and sprinkle cheese over each.

Tuna Pasta

Side Dishes

Baked Potatoes

Yield: 4 servings **Prep Time:** 5 minutes **Total Time:** 60 minutes

Ingredients

- 4 (6–8-oz) russet potatoes, roughly 6 to 8 ounces each
- Extra-virgin olive oil
- Kosher salt and pepper, to taste

For the toppings:

- Sour cream
- Crumbled bacon
- Chopped chives
- Shredded cheddar cheese
- Unsalted butter

Directions

1. Preheat the oven to 425°F. Line a baking sheet with aluminum foil.
2. Wash the potatoes thoroughly with a vegetable brush. If you don't have a vegetable brush, use a damp paper towel. Pat them dry with a paper towel.
3. Pierce each potato several times with a fork (this will allow steam to escape while the potatoes bake so they don't explode). Using your fingers, coat each potato with olive oil. Sprinkle salt on each potato.
4. Place the potatoes on the prepared baking sheet. Bake for 50–60 minutes, until a fork inserted into the potato goes in easily.
5. Slice the top of each potato from end to end. Add salt and pepper to the inside of each potato.
6. Add your desired toppings.

Notes: I think the most important step here is to thoroughly wash the potatoes, since the skins may be consumed.
If you like living on the wild side, you can coat the potatoes with bacon grease instead of olive oil.

Now You're Cooking!

Green Beans with Almonds

Yield: 4 servings   **Prep Time:** 15 minutes   **Total Time:** 30 minutes

Ingredients

- ⅓ cup slivered almonds
- 1 lb fresh green beans, trimmed and snapped in half
- 1 Tbsp unsalted butter
- 1 Tbsp extra-virgin olive oil
- ½ cup sliced red onion
- 2 cloves garlic, minced
- 1 tsp dried thyme
- 1 tsp dried basil
- Kosher salt and pepper, to taste
- ¼ cup grated Parmesan cheese

Directions

1. Preheat the oven to 350°F.
2. Place the almonds in an ovenproof skillet and bake for 5–10 minutes, just until golden brown.
3. Bring a large pot of water to a boil. Blanch the green beans in boiling water for 3 minutes.
4. Remove the beans and drain the water from the pot. Reduce the heat to medium-high and add the butter and olive oil to the pot. Add the onions and cook for 3 minutes.
5. Add the beans back to the pot along with the garlic, thyme, and basil. Sauté for 2 minutes.
6. Season with salt and pepper and toss with toasted almonds and Parmesan.

Green Beans with Almonds

Sautéed Mushrooms and Spinach

Yield: 4 servings **Prep Time:** 10 minutes **Total Time:** 20 minutes

Ingredients

- ¼ cup extra-virgin olive oil
- 2 Tbsp unsalted butter
- 1 lb baby bella mushrooms, sliced
- Half a small sweet onion, sliced (optional)
- 2 cloves garlic, minced
- 2 Tbsp dry red wine
- ½ tsp garlic salt
- Pepper, to taste
- 5 lb spinach
- ¼ tsp nutmeg

Directions

1. Heat the olive oil and butter in a large skillet over medium-high heat. Add the mushrooms and onions (if using) and cook for 4 minutes, stirring frequently. Add the garlic, wine, garlic salt, and pepper, and cook for 2 minutes.
2. Reduce the heat to medium and add the spinach and nutmeg. Cook, stirring, until all the spinach is wilted.

*Sautéed Mushrooms
and Spinach*

Flava Beans

Yield: 10 servings

Prep Time: 10 minutes

Total Time: 1 hour and 15 minutes (plus 8 hours to soak the beans)

Ingredients

- 1 lb dried baby lima beans
- ¼ cup (4 Tbsp) unsalted butter
- 1 medium yellow onion, finely chopped
- 2 cloves garlic, minced
- 4 cups water, or as needed
- 4 teaspoons Better Than Bouillon vegetable soup base
- 1 tsp dried oregano
- 1 tsp dried rosemary
- 1 tsp dried thyme
- 1 teaspoon kosher salt
- ½ teaspoon pepper

Directions

1. Place the lima beans in a large pot and cover with water by about 2 inches. Let soak for about 8 hours. Strain.
2. Melt the butter in a large pot over medium heat. Add the onions and sauté for 3 minutes. Add the garlic and cook for 1 minute.
3. Add the beans and the water to the pan. Water should cover the beans by at least ½ inch. Add the soup base, oregano, rosemary, thyme, salt, and pepper.
4. Bring to a boil. Cover, reduce the heat to low, and let simmer for 45 minutes, until the beans are tender.
5. Remove from the heat and let rest for 15–20 minutes prior to serving.

Note: If you don't want to blow people away (and not in a good way) after eating beans, make sure you soak the dried beans in water for eight hours or overnight in the fridge.

Flava Beans

Steamed Zucchini and Yellow Squash

Yield: 4 servings **Prep Time:** 5 minutes **Total Time:** 20 minutes

Ingredients

- 1 tsp Better Than Bouillon vegetable soup base (or any flavor you prefer)
- 2 medium zucchinis, cut into ½-inch slices
- 2 medium yellow squash, cut into ½-inch slices
- 1 tsp minced garlic
- 2 Tbsp chopped fresh thyme or 2 tsp dried thyme
- 1 tsp extra-virgin olive oil
- Kosher salt and pepper, to taste

Directions

1. Place the soup base and an inch of water in the bottom of a steamer and bring to a boil.
2. In a large bowl, combine the zucchini and yellow squash with the minced garlic.
3. Place the squash mixture into a steamer basket, then place it in the pot. Let steam for 2–3 minutes. Sprinkle with the thyme and steam another 3 minutes.
4. Transfer the vegetables to a large bowl.
5. Drizzle the olive oil over the veggies and toss to coat. Season with salt and pepper to taste.

Note: If you don't have a steamer insert, you can put 1–2 inches of water in the bottom of the pot and bring to a boil. Add the veggies and cover with a lid.

Steamed Zucchini and Yellow Squash

Easy Mac and Cheese

That familiar blue box doesn't have to enter your home when you learn how easily and quickly you can make mac and cheese yourself. The beauty of this recipe is the potential to make it as cheesy and flavorful as you want.

Yield: 4 servings **Prep Time:** 15 minutes **Total Time:** 35 minutes

Ingredients

- 1 tsp kosher salt
- 8 oz elbow macaroni
- 8–10 cups water
- ¼ cup (4 Tbsp) butter
- ¼ cup all-purpose flour
- 2 cups whole milk
- ⅓ cup Big Daddy Mac Mix, or 2½ cups grated cheese of your choice
- ½ tsp seasoned salt
- ¼ tsp pepper

Directions

1. Bring a large pot of water and the salt to a boil in a large pot. Make sure there is enough water in the pan to cover the pasta. Add the pasta and cook for 8 minutes. Strain.
2. Meanwhile, melt the butter in a medium-size saucepan. Add the flour and cook, stirring constantly, until light brown to make a roux.
3. Whisk in the milk. Stir in the mac mix, seasoned salt, and pepper. Cook, stirring, for 2 minutes. Remove from heat.
4. Add the pasta to the sauce and stir to combine thoroughly.

Note: *Unless you have picky eaters at your house, try experimenting to create your own version. There is no rule that elbow macaroni must be used; try a different pasta shape like bowtie pasta. Also, try using your favorite cheese(s) instead of the powdered cheese. This is an excellent way to use up some of the leftover cheese like Gouda, mozzarella, or Parmesan in your fridge.*

Easy Mac and Cheese

Honey-Butter Corn Muffins

Yield: 12 servings **Prep Time:** 10 minutes **Total Time:** 35 minutes

Ingredients

- 2 (8.5-oz) boxes Jiffy corn muffin mix
- 2 large eggs
- ²/₃ cup whole milk
- ½ cup sour cream
- ½ cup (1 stick) unsalted butter, melted, plus more for pan
- 2–3 Tbsp honey
- 1 (15.25-oz) can whole-kernel corn, strained (optional)

Directions

1. Preheat the oven to 400°F. Grease a 12-cup muffin pan.
2. In a large mixing bowl, stir all the ingredients together.
3. Fill each muffin cup two-thirds full.
4. Bake for 20–25 minutes, until golden brown.

Note: If you decide to use a specialty pan rather than a traditional muffin pan, use the recommended baking time for that pan or check periodically until golden brown.

Smoky Greens

Yield: 6 to 8 servings **Prep Time:** 10 minutes **Total Time:** 2 hours and 20 minutes

Ingredients

- 1–2 Tbsp extra-virgin olive oil
- 4 strips turkey or pork bacon
- 1 medium sweet onion, chopped
- 4 cloves garlic, minced
- 2 quarts low-sodium vegetable broth
- 1 smoked turkey wing
- 2 Tbsp apple cider vinegar
- 1 Tbsp sugar or maple syrup
- 2 Tbsp smoked paprika
- ½–1 tsp red pepper flakes
- ½ tsp baking soda
- ½ cup (1 stick) unsalted butter
- 2 lb prewashed and shredded collard greens
- Kosher salt, to taste

Directions

1. In a large stockpot over medium-high heat, heat 1 Tbsp of the olive oil (only if using turkey bacon) and the bacon; cook until crispy. Remove the bacon from the pot and place on a cutting board. Chop coarsely and set aside.
2. Heat the remaining 1 Tbsp olive oil (or rendered bacon fat if using pork bacon) in the pot. Add the onions and sauté for 4 minutes. Add the garlic and cook for 1 minute. Add the vegetable broth and turkey wing, reduce the heat, and simmer for 1 hour.
3. Add the vinegar, sugar, smoked paprika, red pepper flakes, baking soda, and butter along with the collard greens to the pot. Bring to a boil. Reduce heat and simmer for 1 hour. Add salt if needed.
4. Top collard greens with reserved bacon to serve.

Note: The smoked turkey wings should provide enough salt to season your greens. If you feel more is needed, I suggest adding ½ tsp at a time. You can always add, but you can never take it away.

Roasted Asparagus

Yield: 2 to 4 servings **Prep Time:** 10 minutes **Total Time:** 25 minutes

Ingredients

- 1 (about 1-lb) bunch thick asparagus spears, trimmed
- 1 tsp extra-virgin olive oil
- 1 Tbsp Dijon mustard
- 1 tsp minced garlic
- 2 Tbsp chopped fresh tarragon or 2 tsp dried tarragon
- ½ tsp sea salt
- ¼ tsp pepper
- ½ cup shredded Parmesan or Pecorino Romano cheese

Directions

1. Preheat the oven to 425°F.
2. In a medium-size bowl, combine the asparagus, olive oil, mustard, garlic, tarragon, salt, and pepper. Toss to coat.
3. Spread the asparagus on a baking sheet. Bake for 10 minutes. Sprinkle the cheese on top and bake for another 5 minutes.

Note: Trim the asparagus by cutting off the woody ends of each stalk. Alternatively, you can place your thumb and forefinger on the cut end of the asparagus and bend it until it snaps.

Yellow Rice

This recipe was inspired by a unique way of cooking brown rice posted on Saveur's website. To cook the perfect brown rice, you prepare it just as you would pasta! Adding turmeric to the mix yields the perfect yellow color. You will need a fine-mesh strainer or rice-washing bowl to rinse the rice.

Yield: 4 servings
Prep Time: 10 minutes
Total Time: 65 minutes

Ingredients

- *12 cups water*
- *4 tsp L.B. Jamison's chicken-flavored soup base or Better than Bouillon vegetable soup base*
- *1 tsp turmeric*
- *1 tsp Sazon Tropical with coriander and annatto (optional)*
- *1 cup brown rice, rinsed with cold water*

Directions

1. Bring the water, soup base, turmeric, and Sazon to a boil in a covered large pot.
2. Add the rice and cook, uncovered, for 30 minutes. Strain.
3. Place the rice back into the pot, and let sit for 10 minutes, covered and off the heat (this allows the rice to steam).
4. Fluff the rice with a fork prior to serving.

Note: *Why turn brown rice into yellow rice? Turmeric is believed to have many health benefits, from helping to fight cancer and depression to easing PMS symptoms and menstrual cramps. TMI?*

Sautéed Cabbage

Yield: 6 servings **Prep Time:** 10 minutes **Total Time:** 30 minutes

Ingredients

- 2 Tbsp extra-virgin olive oil
- 1 Tbsp unsalted butter
- 1 medium red onion, thinly sliced
- ½ tsp minced garlic
- 1 small (about 2 lb) head cabbage, cored and thinly sliced
- 1¼ tsp kosher salt, divided
- ½ plus ⅛ tsp pepper
- 2 Tbsp apple cider vinegar
- ½ Tbsp Dijon mustard or stone-ground mustard

Directions

1. Heat the olive oil and butter in a large skillet or sauté pan over medium-high heat. Add the onions; sauté for 5 minutes. Add the garlic; sauté for 1 minute. Add the cabbage, 1 teaspoon salt, and ½ tsp pepper; sauté for 10 minutes.
2. In a bowl combine the vinegar, mustard, ¼ tsp salt, and ⅛ tsp pepper.
3. Pour the vinegar mixture to the pan. Stir to combine, and heat through.

Note: Not all cabbages are equally sized. My small may not be small to you. If you don't have a food scale, you should only use what can comfortably fit in a large pan. Any remaining cabbage can be used later for coleslaw.

Mother Dear, Can We Get Outside Food?

I know there are days when you and/or your family get tired of home-cooked meals and start longing for takeout—but don't always give in! Sure, there will be days when you want a quick treat after a long day or as a celebration, but you can create restaurant-quality meals at home and get the family or friends to help prepare them. You may even find that your home-cooked "takeout" tastes better than food from your favorite restaurant.

Oreo Milkshake

Yield: 2 servings   **Prep Time:** 5 minutes   **Total Time:** 5 minutes

Ingredients

- 2 cups vanilla ice cream
- ¼ cup whole milk
- 1 tsp vanilla extract
- 6 Oreo cookies
- Whipped cream (optional)

Directions

1. Combine the ice cream, milk, vanilla, and cookies in a high-speed blender. Blend until smooth.
2. Pour the milkshake into two tall glasses.
3. If desired, top with whipped cream.

Air-Fried Sweet Potato Fries

Yield: 2 servings **Prep Time:** 10 minutes **Total Time:** 25 minutes

Ingredients

- 2 medium-size sweet potatoes, peeled and cut into ¼-in slices
- 1 Tbsp cornstarch
- 2 tsp extra-virgin olive oil
- ¼ tsp garlic powder
- ¼ tsp smoked paprika
- ½ tsp Lawry's seasoned salt
- 1 tsp cinnamon (optional)
- 1 Tbsp packed light brown sugar (optional)

Directions

1. Preheat the air fryer to 390°F.
2. Place the potato slices in a large bowl and sprinkle with the cornstarch; toss to coat.
3. Mix the olive oil, garlic powder, smoked paprika, seasoned salt, and cinnamon and sugar (if using) in a small bowl.
4. Drizzle the seasoned oil over the fries; toss to coat.
5. Spread the fries evenly on a baking sheet and bake for 15 minutes, until crispy.

Note: You don't have to soak sweet potatoes in water because they don't contain as much starch as white potatoes.

McDowell's Breakfast Burrito

No need to go to a drive-through when you can easily make your own breakfast burritos. You can make them as spicy as you want by adjusting the seasonings and the type of diced tomatoes used (e.g., with hot, serrano, or chipotle chilies).

Yield: 6 servings **Prep Time:** 10 minutes **Total Time:** 20 minutes

Ingredients

- ½ lb homemade Turkey Breakfast Sausage (page 36), Jennie-O All-Natural Turkey Sausage, or Jimmy Dean Premium Pork Regular Sausage Roll
- 1 Tbsp extra-virgin olive oil
- Half a medium yellow onion, diced
- 8 large eggs
- Half of a 10-oz can Ro-Tel diced tomatoes with green chilies, drained
- ¼ tsp kosher salt
- Dash (⅛ tsp) pepper
- 3 slices American cheese, cut in half
- 6 (10-inch) flour tortillas, warmed
- Salsa, for serving (optional)

Directions

1. Heat a medium-size nonstick skillet over medium heat. Add the sausage and cook, breaking it up with a spatula, until browned. Remove to a large bowl and wipe out the pan with a paper towel.
2. Heat the olive oil in the same skillet over medium heat. Add the onion and sauté 3 minutes, until softened.
3. Add the eggs, tomatoes with chilies, salt, and pepper to the bowl with the sausage; stir to combine.
4. Pour the egg mixture into the skillet with the onions and cook, stirring frequently, until cooked. Remove from heat.
5. Place 2 Tbsp of the sausage and egg mixture in the middle of each tortilla. Put a half cheese slice on top, fold the bottom up over the filling and the sides over the middle, and continue rolling.
6. Serve with salsa, if desired

Note: *If using pork sausage, drain excess grease before adding to the egg mixture.*

McDowell's Breakfast Burrito

Southwestern Egg Rolls

Yield: 4 servings **Prep Time:** 10 minutes **Total Time:** 26 minutes

Ingredients

- 1 cup fresh spinach
- 2 tsp extra-virgin olive oil
- 1 cup diced cooked chicken breast
- ½ cup canned seasoned black beans, rinsed and strained
- ½ cup Green Giant Mexicorn
- 1 tsp cumin
- 1 tsp garlic powder
- 1 tsp chili powder
- 1 tsp kosher salt
- ¾ cup shredded pepper Jack cheese
- 4 (6-inch) flour tortillas
- Avocado Ranch Dressing (page 61), for dipping

Directions

1. Preheat the air fryer to 400°F.
2. Heat the olive oil in a medium-size skillet over medium high heat. Add the spinach and sauté until wilted, about 1 minute. Let cool. Squeeze the spinach dry using a strainer or potato ricer. If you don't have these items, place the spinach between paper towels.
3. Mix the spinach, chicken, beans, corn, spices, and cheese in a medium-size bowl.
4. Place 2 Tbsp of the mixture in the center of each tortilla. Grab the bottom edge of the tortilla and roll it tightly over the filling. Fold in the sides and continue to roll up.
5. Place them on a rack and bake for 8 minutes, until tortillas are crispy, flipping halfway through.
6. Serve with Avocado Ranch Dressing.

Southwestern Egg Rolls

Air-Fried French Fries

Yield: 2 servings **Prep Time:** 15 minutes **Total Time:** 45 minutes (plus 1 hour to soak the potatoes)

Ingredients
- *2 russet potatoes*
- *Olive oil spray*
- *1 tsp dried rosemary*
- *Kosher salt and pepper, to taste*

Directions
1. Peel the potatoes and cut into ¼-inch slices. Place them in a bowl and cover with water. Chill in the fridge for at least 1 hour.
2. Strain, rinse the fries, and pat dry with paper towels.
3. Preheat the air fryer to 375°F.
4. Place the potatoes in a medium-size bowl and spritz 2–3 times with olive oil. Sprinkle them with rosemary, salt, and pepper.
5. Place in the air fryer and cook for 12–15 minutes, shaking or flipping halfway through the cooking time.

French Fries and Sweet Potato Fries

Shrimp Teriyaki Stir-Fry

Yield: 4 servings **Prep Time:** 15 minutes **Total Time:** 40 minutes

Ingredients

- 2 Tbsp extra-virgin olive oil
- 1 lb shrimp, peeled and deveined
- ½ tsp kosher salt
- ¼ tsp pepper
- ½ tsp minced garlic
- 1 (10-oz) bag frozen stir-fry vegetables, preferably Asian-style
- 1 tsp L.B. Jamison's chicken-flavored soup base or Better Than Bouillon sautéed onion
- 1 cup plus 2 Tbsp water
- 1 Tbsp cornstarch
- ½ tsp ground ginger
- 2 Tbsp packed light brown sugar
- ¼ cup low-sodium soy sauce
- 2 Tbsp mirin
- 4 cups cooked brown or white rice, for serving

Directions

1. In a large skillet, heat the olive oil over medium-high heat. Add the shrimp and sprinkle with salt and pepper. Cook for 2 minutes on each side; add the garlic during the last minute of cooking. Remove the shrimp to a plate.
2. Add the vegetables, soup base, and 1 cup water to the skillet; stir to combine, and bring to a boil. Cover the skillet and reduce the heat to medium; cook for 5–6 minutes.
3. While the vegetables are cooking, stir the cornstarch and 2 Tbsp water together in a small bowl. Add the ginger, brown sugar, soy sauce, and mirin to the bowl. Set aside.
4. Reduce the heat to medium-low and add the shrimp back to the skillet.
5. Pour the cornstarch mixture over the shrimp and vegetables. Cook, stirring, until heated through.
6. Serve over rice.

Note: Mirin (MEER-in) is a rice wine seasoning. You can find it in the Asian aisle of your grocery store or online.

Shrimp Teriyaki Stir-Fry

Air-Fried Shrimp Hushpuppies

Yield: 12 servings **Prep Time:** 15 minutes **Total Time:** 50 minutes

Ingredients

- 1 (8.5-oz) box Jiffy Cornbread mix
- ¼ cup all-purpose flour
- 1 tsp kosher salt
- ¼ tsp cayenne pepper
- ¼ tsp garlic powder
- ¼ tsp onion powder
- ½ tsp smoked paprika
- ¼ cup Pictsweet Farms seasoning blend (diced green and red peppers, onions, and celery)
- ⅓ cup whole milk
- 1 large egg, beaten
- ½ cup grated cheddar cheese
- ½ lb peeled cooked shrimp, chopped

Directions

1. Preheat the air fryer to 360°F.
2. In a large bowl, whisk together the cornbread mix, flour, salt, cayenne pepper, garlic and onion powders, and smoked paprika. Add the seasoning blend, milk, egg, cheese, and shrimp and stir to combine. Let mixture rest for 5 minutes.
3. Line the bottom of the air fryer basket with parchment paper made specifically for the air fryer, or aluminum foil. If using foil, coat it with nonstick spray.
4. Using a tablespoon or cookie scoop, drop the dough onto the parchment or foil. Make sure the hush puppies don't touch each other. Cook for 5 minutes, flip, and cook another 5 minutes.
5. Hushpuppies will last 1 week in the fridge and up to 1 month in the freezer (if you don't eat them all first!).

Notes: Check to make sure the cooked shrimp is thoroughly deveined.
If you can't find the Pictweet Farms chopped seasoning blend, look for the Pictsweet Farms Tri-Colored Pepper and Onion Medley and add chopped fresh celery.

Shrimp Fried Rice

Yield: 4 servings   **Prep Time:** 15 minutes   **Total Time:** 40 minutes

Ingredients

- 3 tsp canola oil, divided
- 2 large eggs, beaten
- 1 lb medium shrimp, peeled and deveined
- ½ tsp lemon pepper seasoning
- ½ cup shredded carrots
- ½ cup sliced green onions
- 1 (14-oz) can bean sprouts, strained
- 1 tsp minced garlic
- ½ tsp ground ginger
- 4 cups day-old cooked jasmine rice
- Kosher salt and pepper, to taste
- ¼ cup low-sodium soy sauce
- 1 tsp toasted sesame oil

Directions

1. Heat 1 tsp of the oil in a large skillet over medium-high heat. Add the eggs and scramble. Remove the eggs to a plate.
2. Add the remaining 2 tsp oil to the skillet. Add the shrimp and sprinkle with the lemon pepper seasoning. Cook for 4 minutes, flipping halfway. Remove to the plate with the eggs.
3. Add the carrots, green onions, and bean sprouts to the skillet; cook for 2–3 minutes. Add the garlic and ginger; cook for 1 minute. Add the rice and cook, stirring, for about 5 minutes to reheat. Add the shrimp and eggs back to the skillet. Season with salt and pepper.
4. Pour in the soy sauce and sesame oil. Stir to combine.

Time for a Kickback!
Let's Throw a Casual Dinner Party

Do you want to host a small casual dinner party for friends and/or family? You don't have to spend money on catering. This chapter will show you how to plan for the gathering, giving you the freedom to enjoy yourself along with your guests.

Menu

- Moscato Punch
- French Onion Soup
- Mixed Greens with Balsamic Vinaigrette
- Herbed Cream Cheese Crescent Rolls
- Scalloped Potatoes
- Roasted Chicken Breasts with Lemon-Basil Sauce
- Simply Delicious Apple Dump Cake

Dinner parties are a lot of fun but can be a lot of work for the host/hostess. With some careful planning, you can spend more time with your guests instead of working in the kitchen all evening. Depending on how many guests you invite, you may need to double some recipes. As a general rule, you want to invite no more than eight people to a dinner party so you won't feel overwhelmed.

Work Plan
One month to three weeks ahead

- Determine theme: Will it be casual or fancy?
- Create guest list and send out invitations. Make sure the invitations include an RSVP deadline of one week before the date of the party, as well as a line for guests to note any food allergies or restrictions..
- Start collecting all decorations, serving platters, tablecloths, and utensils. If you're missing anything you need, purchase (or borrow) it today.
- Start planning your menu.

Two to three weeks ahead:

- Create music playlist.
- Clean and iron napkins and tablecloths.

One week ahead:

- RSVP deadline.
- Finalize menu, adjusting according to guests' dietary restrictions.
- Read through the recipes on the menu.
- Confirm which ingredients you already have.
- Create your grocery list and check it twice. (See page 125)
- If there are any nonperishable items on your grocery list purchase/order them now.
- Confirm all serving platters and utensils.

Three days before party:

- Clean the house. Depending on how many guests you've invited, make sure multiple bathrooms are clean. If using a master bathroom, remove personal items (you don't want your friends all in your business or, even worse, have your Vicodin or Percocet turn up missing!).
- Depending on the time of year, gather extra hangers if using a closet to store guest coats and/or purses, or designate a bed to store them on.

One day before party:

- Light cleaning: dust, vacuum, mop floors.
- Set the table.
- Purchase flowers.
- If you have pets, consider taking them to a pet day care (you may have guests that are allergic or afraid).
- Make the French onion soup, but save the croutons and cheese for tomorrow. Let cool then store in fridge.
- Chill the wine, pineapple juice, and ginger ale in fridge.
- Prepare the scalloped potatoes (don't cook yet), and store in fridge.
- Prepare and cook the chicken breasts with lemon-basil sauce. Let cool then store in fridge.

Two hours before guests arrive:

- Prepare the salad and vinaigrette. Place in the fridge to chill.
- Prepare the Moscato punch and place in the fridge. Place scalloped potatoes on counter, if using a glass dish (you don't want to put a cold vessel in a hot oven—bad things could happen).

One hour before guests arrive:

- Cook scalloped potatoes.
- Prepare the dump cake (don't cook yet), cover, and let it sit on the counter.
- Get dressed.

Thirty minutes before guests arrive:

- Start reheating any food that was previously made and chilled.
- The onion soup should be reheated in a pot on the stove.
- Reheat the chicken: Add one cup of chicken broth to the bottom of the baking dish and cover with aluminum foil; heat in the oven at 350°F for 20 minutes.
- Prepare the crescent rolls and place on the baking sheet. Store in the fridge until ready to bake.

Fifteen minutes before:

- Add ice to the Moscato punch.
- Place sodas (or store-bought non-alcoholic punch) and/or water next to the Moscato punch.
- Take pictures of everything! Post to social media.

Just before sitting down to dinner:

- Divide the soup equally into six bowls (or per the number of guests) and put the croutons and cheese on top. Place the bowls on a baking sheet and place under the broiler to melt the cheese. A common rookie mistake is to walk away from the broiler. Don't do it! You may even want to leave the door open to keep an eye on it. Your guests won't appreciate burnt cheese. It only takes a few minutes to melt the cheese. The soup is already hot.

While enjoying the soup:

- Adjust the oven temp to 375°F. Place the crescent rolls into the oven. Bake for 10 to 12 minutes. Wrap the bread in a towel and place in a bowl or basket once done to keep them warm.

While enjoying dinner:

- Preheat the oven to 350°F then place the apple dump cake in the oven. The aroma of a fresh baked cake will only increase anticipation for the dessert while your guests are mingling and enjoying dinner. If you feel that waiting until just before guests arrive to bake the dessert would be too stressful feel free to prepare it the night before and reheat at 300°F during dinner.

Dinner Party Grocery List

- 4 (6-oz) chicken breasts
- 1½ cups grated Gruyere cheese
- ½ cup grated sharp cheddar cheese
- 8 oz grated Parmesan cheese
- 5 oz shaved Parmesan cheese
- 1 (8-oz) package cream cheese
- Unsalted butter
- 16 oz. heavy cream
- ½ gallon vanilla ice cream (don't judge!)
- 8 lemons
- 6 limes
- 1 head garlic
- 4 yellow onions
- 8 oz mushrooms
- Carrots
- 1 cucumber
- 1 bag mixed greens
- 1 bag baby spinach
- Fresh thyme
- 2 russet potatoes
- 1 (4.5-oz) jar minced garlic
- Garlic paste
- 1 (5-oz) bag seasoned croutons
- 16 oz Red Rock ginger ale or Canada Dry Bold ginger ale
- 24 oz pineapple juice
- Chicken broth
- Honey
- Extra-virgin olive oil
- Balsamic vinegar
- Better than Bouillon sautéed onion or seasoned vegetable soup base
- Better than Bouillon chicken soup base
- 1 cup walnuts
- 1 (15.25-oz) box yellow cake mix
- 2 (8-oz) cans refrigerated crescent rolls
- 2 (21-oz) cans apple pie filling
- Light brown sugar
- Garlic powder
- Celery seed
- Paprika

- Umami (mushroom) powder
- Cinnamon
- Fresh or ground nutmeg
- Salt-free chicken seasoning
- Dried parsley flakes
- Dried thyme
- Dried basil
- Italian seasoning
- Bay leaves
- Kosher salt
- Pepper
- Cornstarch
- Bread crumbs
- Hidden Valley Ranch salad dressing and seasoning mix
- 1 (750-ml) bottle Moscato wine
- 1 (750-ml) bottle dry white wine (such as sauvignon blanc)

Herbed Cream Cheese Crescent Rolls

Yield: 16 servings (2 rolls each)
Prep Time: 15 minutes
Total Time: 30 minutes

Ingredients

- 1 (8-oz) package cream cheese, softened
- 2 Tbsp Hidden Valley Ranch salad dressing and seasoning mix
- 1 tsp chopped fresh basil or ½ tsp dried basil
- 3 Tbsp unsalted butter, melted
- 1 tsp Italian seasoning
- 2 cloves garlic, minced
- 1 tsp chopped fresh parsley or ½ tsp dried parsley
- 2 (8-oz) cans refrigerated crescent rolls

Directions

1. Preheat the oven to 375°F.
2. In a medium bowl, mix together the cream cheese, dressing mix, and basil.
3. In a small bowl, combine 3 Tbsp of the melted butter, and the Italian seasoning, garlic, and parsley.
4. Unroll and separate the crescent rolls. Spread 1 tsp of the cream cheese mixture evenly along the large end of the roll. Roll up towards the small end, enclosing the filling. Tuck the ends under and pinch the edges to ensure filling is sealed in.
5. Brush the tops of the rolls with the garlic butter.
6. Place the rolls on an ungreased baking sheet. Bake for 10–12 minutes

Moscato Punch

Yield: 8 servings   **Prep Time:** 10 minutes   **Total Time:** 10 minutes

Ingredients

- 1 (750-ml) bottle chilled Moscato wine
- 16 oz chilled Red Rock ginger ale or Canada Dry Bold ginger ale
- 3 cups chilled pineapple juice
- ¼ cup fresh lemon juice (3–5 lemons)
- ¼ cup fresh lime juice (4–6 limes)
- 4 cups ice cubes

Directions

1. Pour Moscato, ginger ale, pineapple juice, and lemon and lime juices into a pitcher or large punch bowl. Stir to combine. Add ice. Serve immediately.

Moscato Punch

French Onion Soup

Yield: 6 servings | **Prep Time:** 30 minutes | **Total Time:** 90 minutes

Ingredients

- 1 Tbsp extra-virgin olive oil
- 4 yellow onions, sliced
- 2 Tbsp balsamic vinegar
- 2 Tbsp packed light brown sugar
- ⅓ cup dry white wine
- 6 cups plus 2 Tbsp water, divided
- 3 Tbsp Better Than Bouillon sautéed onion or seasoned vegetable soup base
- 1 tsp garlic powder
- ¼ tsp parsley flakes
- ⅛ tsp celery seed
- ⅛ tsp paprika
- ½ tsp umami (mushroom) powder (optional)
- ¼ tsp dried thyme
- ½ tsp kosher salt
- ¼ tsp pepper
- 2 Tbsp cornstarch
- 1 (5-oz) bag seasoned croutons
- 1½ cups grated Gruyère cheese

Directions

1. Heat the olive oil in a large Dutch oven over medium heat. Add the onions and cook for 15 minutes, until soft. Add the vinegar and sugar and cook for an additional 20 minutes, until onions are caramelized. Add the wine and cook until it has evaporated. Remove from heat.
2. Meanwhile, place 6 cups water, the soup base, garlic powder, parsley flakes, celery seed, paprika, umami powder, thyme, salt, and pepper in a high-speed blender. Blend for 5–6 minutes, until hot (the force from the blender should heat the soup).
3. In a small bowl, combine the cornstarch and 2 Tbsp water; stir this into the soup. Let the blender run on low for 1 minute, until the soup is thick; this step should not take more than a couple of minutes. Add the onions to the blender and process on low for 1 minute.
4. Divide the soup among six heatproof bowls. Top each with 5–6 croutons and ¼ cup cheese. Place the bowls on a baking sheet and place under the broiler just long enough to melt the cheese, about 4 minutes (keep an eye on it!).

Mixed Greens with Balsamic Vinaigrette

Yield: 4 servings **Prep Time:** 15 minutes **Total Time:** 20 minutes

Ingredients

- ¼ cup balsamic vinegar
- ¾ cup extra-virgin olive oil
- 1 Tbsp honey
- ½ tsp kosher salt
- ¼ tsp pepper
- 4 cups combination of mixed greens and baby spinach
- ½ cup sliced mushrooms
- ¼ cup shredded carrots
- ½ cucumber, peeled, halved lengthwise, and sliced
- ¼ cup toasted chopped walnuts
- ¼ cup shaved Parmesan cheese

Directions

1. In a medium-size bowl, whisk together the vinegar, oil, honey, salt, and pepper.
2. Place the greens, mushrooms, carrots, and cucumbers in a large bowl.
3. Pour the vinaigrette over the top of the salad; toss to combine.
4. Divide the salad among four bowls. Top each with the walnuts and Parmesan.

Scalloped Potatoes

Yield: 4 to 6 servings
Prep Time: 20 minutes
Total Time: 75 minutes

Ingredients

- 1½ cups heavy cream
- 1 cup chicken broth
- 1 Tbsp Better Than Bouillon roasted chicken soup base
- 2 sprigs fresh thyme
- 2 cloves garlic, minced
- ¼ tsp grated fresh nutmeg or ½ tsp ground nutmeg
- 2 bay leaves
- 1 tsp kosher salt
- ½ tsp pepper
- 2 cups peeled and 1/8-inch-sliced russet potatoes (about 2 potatoes)
- ½ cup grated Parmesan cheese
- 1 Tbsp unsalted butter, melted, plus more for casserole dish
- ¼ cup bread crumbs
- ½ cup grated sharp cheddar cheese

Directions

1. Preheat the oven to 400°F. Coat a 1.5-quart casserole dish or an 8x8-inch baking dish with butter.
2. In a medium saucepan over medium-low heat, heat the cream, broth, soup base, thyme, garlic, nutmeg, bay leaves, salt, and pepper until fragrant, about 5 minutes. Add the sliced potatoes, cover, and cook 10 minutes. Remove from heat.
3. Discard the bay leaves and thyme sprigs. Add Parmesan to the saucepan; stir gently to combine.
4. Transfer the potato mixture to the prepared baking dish.
5. In a small bowl, combine 1 Tbsp melted butter with the bread crumbs and cheddar. Sprinkle the bread crumb mixture over the top of the casserole.
6. Bake for 40 minutes, until browned on top and bubbling.

Scalloped Potatoes

Simply Delicious Apple Dump Cake

My brother once suggested one of his middle school students make a dump cake for his mother on Mother's Day. It wasn't until it got rave reviews that I ever thought about making a dump cake myself. They are so delicious and simple to make.

Yield: 12 servings **Prep Time:** 5 minutes **Total Time:** 65 minutes

Ingredients

- 2 (21-oz) cans apple pie filling
- 2 teaspoons cinnamon
- ½ teaspoon nutmeg
- 1 (15.25-oz) box yellow cake mix
- ½ cup chopped walnuts
- ¾ cup (1½ sticks) butter, cut into 12 slices
- 1 pint vanilla ice cream, for serving

Directions

1. Preheat the oven to 350°F. Coat a 13x9-in baking pan with nonstick cooking spray.
2. Spread the apple pie filling evenly in the pan.
3. In a small bowl, combine the cinnamon and nutmeg.
4. Sprinkle the spice mixture evenly across the top of the filling. Sprinkle the yellow cake mix over the top of the filling; use a spatula to make sure the mix is distributed evenly. Sprinkle the walnuts evenly over the cake mix. Arrange the 12 tablespoons of butter across the top.
5. Bake 45 minutes to 1 hour, until edges are bubbly and the top is golden brown.
6. Serve with ice cream.

Simply Delicious Apple Dump Cake

Roasted Chicken Breasts with Lemon-Basil Sauce

Yield: 4 servings **Prep Time:** 5 minutes **Total Time:** 55 minutes

Ingredients

- 1 Tbsp extra-virgin olive oil
- 4 (6-oz) boneless, skin-on chicken breasts
- 1½ tsp kosher salt, plus more to taste
- ½ tsp pepper, plus more to taste
- 2 tsp garlic paste
- ¼ cup dry white wine or water
- 1 tsp Better Than Bouillon chicken soup base
- 1 Tbsp salt-free chicken seasoning
- Juice of 3 lemons
- 1½ Tbsp honey
- ½ cup heavy cream
- 1 tsp dried basil

Directions

1. Preheat the oven to 350°F.
2. Heat the olive oil in a large skillet over medium-high heat. Sprinkle the chicken with salt and pepper to taste. Place 2 pieces of chicken skin side down in the skillet. Cook for 2–3 minutes on each side until browned. Transfer the browned chicken to a 9x13-inch baking dish or roasting pan. Repeat with the remaining chicken.
3. Bake the chicken for 30 minutes or until the internal temperature reaches 160°F. Remove from the oven and let rest for 5 minutes. (The chicken will continue to cook to 165°F even though it is out of the oven.)
4. Meanwhile, add the garlic paste to the skillet over medium heat; cook for 1 minute. Add the wine or water. Deglaze the pan by cleaning the fond (browned bits) off the bottom with a wooden spoon.
5. Add the chicken base, 1½ tsp salt, ½ tsp pepper, salt-free seasoning, lemon juice, honey, cream, and basil to the skillet. Cook for 2 minutes, until the sauce thickens.
6. Place the chicken on a serving platter and pour the sauce over the top.

Note: You will need to double the recipe for the dinner party if serving more than four people.

Charlene's Favorites

Chicken Liver Pâté

Yield: 14 to 16 servings
Prep Time: 10 minutes
Total Time: 35 minutes (plus 3 hours to soak the livers)

Ingredients

- 1 lb chicken livers
- 2 cups whole milk
- 5 Tbsp unsalted butter, divided
- Half a small yellow onion, chopped
- 2 tsp garlic, minced
- ¼ cup chopped sweet onions
- ½ tsp umami (mushroom) powder (optional)
- ½ tsp onion powder
- ½ tsp garlic powder
- ½ tsp dried rosemary
- 1 tsp balsamic vinegar
- 2 Tbsp Worcestershire sauce
- 1 Tbsp dry sherry
- ½ tsp kosher salt, plus more to taste
- ¼ tsp pepper
- ¼ cup heavy cream
- 1 Tbsp cognac (optional)
- 2 large eggs, hard-boiled
- Crackers or toast points, for serving

Directions

1. Remove the connective tissue from the chicken livers and rinse the livers in a colander. Soak the chicken livers in 2 cups milk for at least 3 hours. Strain. Chop them coarsely.
2. In a medium-size skillet, melt 4 Tbsp butter over medium-high heat. Add the onions and garlic. Cook for 2 minutes. Add the chicken livers, umami powder, onion powder, garlic powder, rosemary, vinegar, Worcestershire sauce, sherry, salt, and pepper to the skillet. Cook for 8–10 minutes, until livers are cooked through. Remove from heat and let cool.
3. Add the contents of the skillet to a food processor and purée until smooth. Add the remaining 1 Tbsp butter, the boiled eggs, cream, and cognac (if using) while processing. Add salt if necessary.
4. Transfer the pâté to a container and put plastic wrap directly on the surface. Place it in the fridge to firm up (at least 6 hours or overnight).
5. Serve with crackers or toast points.

Chicken Liver Pâté

Air-Fried Chicken Livers

Yield: 4 servings

Prep Time: 10 minutes

Total Time: 40 minutes, depending on the size of your air fryer (plus 3 hours to soak the livers)

Ingredients

- 1¼ lb chicken livers
- 2 cups whole milk
- 1 cup all-purpose flour
- 2 large eggs
- ½ cup bread crumbs
- 1 cup Andy's Chicken Breading seasoning (or any seasoning brand of your choice)
- Olive oil spray

Directions

1. Remove the connective tissue from the chicken livers and rinse the livers with water in a colander. Soak the chicken livers in the milk for at least 3 hours in the fridge.
2. Strain, rinse the chicken livers, and pat dry with paper towels. Chop them coarsely.
3. Preheat the air fryer to 390°F.
4. Line up three shallow pans. In the first pan place the flour. Beat the eggs in the second pan. Combine the bread crumbs and breading mix in the third pan. Next to that, place a baking sheet lined with parchment paper.
5. Using one hand to work with the eggs and the other hand to work with the flour and the breading mix, dip each chicken liver in the flour, then the eggs, then the breading mix, placing the livers on the prepared baking sheet as you go. Repeat until all the chicken livers are coated.
6. Spray the livers with olive oil.
7. Place the livers in a single layer in the air fryer. Do not crowd the pan; the livers will need to be cooked in batches. Cook for 5 minutes, then flip and cook for another 5 minutes. Serve hot.

Air-Fried Chicken Livers, Brown Rice, and Steamed Zucchini and Yellow Squash

Lasagna

Yield: 12 servings **Prep Time:** 25 minutes **Total Time:** 90 minutes

Ingredients

- 2 Tbsp extra-virgin olive oil
- ½ lb Italian pork or chicken sausage, casings removed
- ½ lb ground beef or ground chicken
- ½ cup minced yellow onion
- 1 tsp minced garlic
- 1 Tbsp tomato paste
- 2 (52-oz) jars marinara sauce
- 2 large eggs
- ½ tsp kosher salt
- ¼ tsp pepper
- ½ cup shredded Parmesan or Parmigiano-Reggiano cheese
- 6 basil leaves, cut into chiffonade
- 1 (15-oz) container ricotta cheese (2 cups)
- 4 cups shredded mozzarella cheese
- 1 (9-oz) box oven-ready lasagna noodles

Directions

1. Preheat the oven to 375°F. Spray a lasagna pan or deep 9x13-in baking dish with nonstick cooking spray.
2. Heat the olive oil in a large pot over medium heat. Cook the sausage, ground beef, and onions, breaking up the meat, until well browned. Add the garlic and cook for an additional 30 seconds. Spoon or drain off the fat. Stir in the tomato paste and all but 1½ cups of the marinara. Let simmer for 15 minutes. Remove from heat.
3. In a large bowl, beat the eggs. Add the salt, pepper, Parmesan, basil, ricotta, and 2 cups of the mozzarella; stir to combine.
4. Spread the reserved 1½ cups marinara sauce in the bottom of the prepared pan. Arrange 4 of the noodles the long way in the pan, then spread with a third of the ricotta mixture, half of the meat sauce, and 1 cup mozzarella. Layer 4 more noodles the short way (you'll have to cut them to fit), a third of the ricotta mixture, and 1½ cups meat sauce. Layer 4 noodles the long way, and spread with the remaining ricotta mixture and 1 cup of the meat sauce. Layer 4 more noodles the short way, then add the remaining meat sauce. Top with the remaining mozzarella and Parmesan.
5. Spray aluminum foil with cooking spray and cover the pan with it. Bake for 1 hour. Remove the foil and bake 5 more minutes, until browned and bubbling. Cool for 15 minutes before cutting.

Notes: *This recipe is an ideal candidate to make ahead, since lasagna tastes better the next day. To save money, skip the pricier Parmigiano Reggiano and use Parmesan cheese. To chiffonade basil, roll the leaves up like a cigar and slice crosswise.*

Lasagna

Sexy Meatloaf with Brown Sugar Glaze

Yield: 10 servings **Prep Time:** 30 minutes **Total Time:** 90 minutes

Ingredients

- 1 Tbsp olive oil
- 1 carrot, roughly chopped
- Half a medium yellow onion, roughly chopped
- Half a red bell pepper, roughly chopped
- 3 cloves garlic, minced
- 2 lb ground turkey or meatloaf mix (any combo of ground veal, pork, and beef)
- 1 cup Italian bread crumbs
- 1 tsp kosher salt
- ½ tsp pepper
- ½ tsp cayenne pepper
- 1 large egg, lightly beaten

For the glaze:
- 1 cup ketchup
- ½ cup light brown sugar
- 1 tsp cumin
- ¼ tsp hot sauce, such as Texas Pete or Frank's
- ¼ tsp Worcestershire sauce

Directions

1. Preheat the oven to 325°F. Line a baking sheet with parchment paper.
2. Pulse the carrot, onion, and bell pepper in a food processor until finely chopped.
3. Put the olive oil, vegetables, and the garlic in a skillet over medium heat, and sweat until the vegetables are soft, about 5 to 10 minutes. Let cool.
4. In a large bowl, use your hands to combine the cooled vegetables with the ground meat and bread crumbs. Season with salt, pepper, and cayenne. Add the egg, combining with your hands.
5. Form the mixture into a loaf shape and place on the prepared baking sheet (or you can use a meatloaf pan).
6. If you have an oven-safe meat thermometer, place it in the top of the meatloaf. Be careful not to let it touch the bottom of the pan. Set the thermometer to 155°F. Bake for 30 minutes.
7. Meanwhile, make the glaze: Combine the ketchup, brown sugar, cumin, hot sauce, and Worcestershire sauce.
8. Take the meatloaf out of the oven and brush with the glaze, using it all. Return to the oven and bake for another 30 minutes, until the internal temperature reaches 155°F. Remove the meatloaf from the oven and let it rest for 10-15 minutes.

Sexy Meatloaf with Brown Sugar Glaze

Charlene's Front Porch Lemonade

Yield: 16 servings   **Prep Time:** 10 minutes   **Total Time:** 55 minutes

Ingredients

- 2 lb fresh strawberries, hulled
- 2 cups sugar
- 1 thumb-size piece fresh ginger, peeled
- 1 cup fresh basil leaves
- 2 cups fresh lemon juice
- 1 gallon cold water or Sprite

Directions

1. Place the strawberries in a large skillet, sprinkle them with the sugar, and add the ginger and basil.
2. Cook for about 10 minutes on low heat. Discard the ginger. Take the skillet off the heat and let steep for 30 minutes.
3. Pour contents of the skillet into a high-speed blender and purée until smooth.
4. Mix the strawberry-basil purée with lemon juice and water or Sprite.

Note: For Back Porch Lemonade, add 1 cup of vodka or limoncello to the recipe above.

Charlene's Front Porch Lemonade

Spiced Hot Chocolate

Yield: 6 servings **Prep Time:** 3 minutes **Total Time:** 8 minutes

Ingredients

- 4 cups milk or almond milk
- ¼ cup sugar
- ¼ cup Hershey's cocoa powder
- 1 dash kosher salt
- ¼ tsp cloves
- ¼ tsp cardamom
- ½ tsp cinnamon
- ¼ tsp nutmeg
- 4 oz milk chocolate, chopped
- ½ tsp vanilla extract

Directions

1. Mix the milk, sugar, cocoa powder, salt, and spices in a saucepan. Heat over medium-high heat, stirring frequently, until warm. Do NOT let it boil.
2. Stir in the milk chocolate until it dissolves.
3. Remove the pot from the heat, and add the vanilla. Serve immediately.

Desserts

Banana Rum Cake

Yield: 12 to 16 servings **Prep Time:** 10 minutes **Total Time:** 1 hour 10 minutes

Ingredients

- 1 cup coarsely chopped macadamia or walnuts
- 1 (15.25-oz) box yellow cake mix
- 1 (5.1-oz) box instant banana pudding mix
- 4 large eggs
- 1 tsp vanilla extract
- ½ cup dark rum
- ¾ cup mashed ripe bananas (about 1 ½ bananas)
- ½ cup water
- ¼ cup (4 Tbsp) unsalted butter, melted

For the glaze:

- ½ cup packed light brown sugar
- ¼ cup powdered sugar
- 2 Tbsp water
- ¼ cup (4 Tbsp) unsalted butter
- ¼ cup dark rum
- 1 tsp banana extract

Directions

1. Preheat the oven to 350°F with a rack in the center position.
2. Grease a Bundt pan thoroughly with nonstick spray, then flour the pan. Sprinkle the chopped nuts in the bottom of the pan.
3. Place the cake mix, pudding mix, eggs, vanilla, rum, bananas, water, and butter in a large mixing bowl. With an electric or stand mixer, combine the ingredients on low speed until blended. Increase the speed to medium and beat 2–3 minutes more.
4. Pour the batter into the prepared pan. Bake the cake until a toothpick inserted in the middle comes out clean or the cake springs back when pressed with your finger, 50–60 minutes.
5. Place the cake on a wire rack to cool in the pan.
6. Meanwhile, make the glaze: Combine the sugars, water, and butter in a saucepan over medium-high heat and boil for 3 minutes. Add the rum and boil for 2 minutes; remove from heat. Stir in the banana extract.
7. Poke holes in the top of the cake with a toothpick. Pour half of the glaze over the cake while the cake is still in the pan. Once the cake cools completely, invert it onto a plate or a cake board. Pour the remaining glaze over the cake.

Banana Rum Cake, Brown Sugar Pound Cake, and 7UP Pound Cake

7Up Pound Cake

Baking a cake mix without eggs or oil? I know it sounds strange, but it works!

Yield: 8 servings **Prep Time:** 5 minutes **Total Time:** 60 minutes

Ingredients

- 1 (16-oz) box Betty Crocker pound cake mix
- 1 mini (7.5-oz) can or 7/8 cup 7UP
- 1 tsp vanilla extract
- 1 tsp lemon extract

For the lemon glaze (optional):

- ½ cup water
- ½ cup granulated sugar
- 1 Tbsp powdered sugar
- 1 Tbsp unsalted butter
- 2 tsp lemon extract

Directions

1. Preheat the oven to 350°F. Spray a pan (see chart on package for info on pans; I use a 9x5-inch loaf pan) with Baker's Joy (baking spray with flour).
2. Beat the cake mix, soda, vanilla, and lemon extract in a medium-size bowl until smooth.
3. Bake as directed (in the 9x5-inch pan, it bakes for 50–55 minutes).
4. About 5 minutes before the cake comes out of the oven, make the lemon glaze: In a medium-size saucepan, bring the water and granulated sugar to a boil. Add the powdered sugar, butter, and lemon extract. Stir and continue boiling for 1 minute. Remove from heat.
5. Let the cake cool for 20 minutes in the pan on a wire rack. Place the cake on a platter and spoon the glaze over it while it's still warm.

Note: Reading is fundamental. Make sure you use a mini 7UP can, NOT a regular-size can of soda, for this recipe.

Sweet Potato Pie

Yield: 6 to 8 servings **Prep Time:** 20 minutes **Total Time:** 1 hour and 30 minutes

Ingredients

For the pie shell:
- 40 Biscoff cookies
- 6 Tbsp unsalted butter, melted

For the filling:
- 1 (15-oz) can sweet potato purée
- ½ cup plus 1 Tbsp sugar
- 2 large eggs, beaten
- 3 Tbsp unsalted butter, melted, divided
- ¼ cup heavy cream or whole milk
- ½ tsp vanilla extract
- ½ tsp cinnamon
- ¼ tsp nutmeg
- 1 tsp all-purpose flour

Directions

1. Preheat the oven to 350°F. Spray a 9-inch pie plate with nonstick cooking spray.
2. Make the pie shell: In a food processor or blender, process the cookies into fine crumbs. Place the crumbs in a medium-size bowl and combine with the melted butter and 1 Tbsp sugar.
3. Pour the crumbs into the prepared pie plate. Using the bottom of a glass or measuring cup, press the mixture into an even layer on the bottom and up the sides of the plate.
4. Bake for 10 minutes, until firm. Remove from oven and let cool.
5. Make the filling: Combine the sweet potato puree, ½ cup sugar, the eggs, melted butter, cream, vanilla, cinnamon, nutmeg, and flour in a large mixing bowl; mix until smooth.
6. Pour the filling into the pie shell. Bake for 60 minutes, until a knife inserted in the center of the filling comes out clean.
7. Cool to room temperature before serving. Any leftovers should be stored in the refrigerator.

Note: If you don't have a food processor, or you feel making your own crust is too daunting or time-consuming, you can use a nine-inch store-bought pie crust from the frozen food section of your grocery store.

Peanut Butter Oatmeal Bars

Yield: 24 servings **Prep Time:** 20 minutes **Total Time:** 50 minutes

Ingredients

- 1 cup all-purpose flour
- 1½ cups old-fashioned oats
- ½ tsp kosher salt
- ½ tsp baking soda
- ½ cup (1 stick) unsalted butter, softened
- ½ cup granulated sugar
- ½ cup packed dark brown sugar
- ¾ cup creamy peanut butter
- 1 large egg
- ½ tsp vanilla extract

For the frosting:

- ½ cup (1 stick) unsalted butter
- ¼ cup smooth peanut butter
- ½ cup chocolate chips
- 2 tsp vanilla extract
- 1 ½ cups powdered sugar
- ¼ cup whole milk
- ½ cup crushed peanut butter Cap'n Crunch cereal

Directions

1. Preheat the oven to 350°F. Coat a 9x13-in baking dish with cooking spray.
2. In a small bowl, combine the flour, oatmeal, salt, and baking soda.
3. In a medium-size bowl, use a hand mixer to cream the butter and sugars together. Add the peanut butter, egg, and vanilla; blend until just combined. Add the dry ingredients; blend until just combined.
4. Spread the batter in the prepared pan. Bake for 20 minutes. Let cool.
5. Make the frosting: In a saucepan over medium-high heat, bring the butter and peanut butter to a boil. Remove from heat.
6. Add the chocolate chips and vanilla. Stir until the chips have melted. Stir in the powdered sugar and milk.
7. Spread the frosting over the cooled bars. Sprinkle the crushed cereal on top of the frosting. Cut into bars.

Chocolate-Dipped Oatmeal Cookies

Yield: 24 cookies **Prep Time:** 25 minutes **Total Time:** 55 minutes

Ingredients

- 2½ cups quick-cooking oats
- 2 cups all-purpose flour
- ½ tsp cinnamon
- 1 tsp kosher salt
- 1 tsp baking soda
- 1 cup granulated sugar
- ½ cup packed light brown sugar
- 1 cup (2 sticks) unsalted butter, softened
- 2 large eggs
- 1 tsp vanilla
- 1 cup pecans (optional)
- 8 oz milk chocolate, chopped
- ½ cup heavy cream

Directions

1. Preheat the oven to 350°F.
2. In a medium-size bowl, combine the flour, cinnamon, salt, and baking soda. Mix well with a wire whisk.
3. In a large bowl, cream the sugars and butter together using an electric mixer. Add the eggs and vanilla; blend until smooth. Add the dry ingredients; blend at low speed until combined. Stir in the oatmeal and nuts, if using.
4. Drop by rounded tablespoons onto ungreased cookie sheets, 2 inches apart.
5. Bake for 14 minutes. Let the cookies cool on a baking sheet for 1–2 minutes then place cookies on a rack to cool.
6. Place the milk chocolate and heavy cream in a microwave-safe bowl. Microwave in 30-second increments, stirring after each, until smooth.
7. Dip each cooled cookie halfway into the chocolate, letting the excess drip into the bowl. Place the cookies on waxed paper to set.

Now You're Cooking!

Bourbon Sea Salt Caramel Turtles

Yield: 24 servings
Prep Time: 15 minutes
Total Time: 25 minutes

Ingredients

- 3 cups pecan halves
- 1 (11-oz) package Kraft caramel squares
- ¼ cup whole milk
- ½ tsp sea salt
- 2 Tbsp bourbon
- 8 oz milk or dark chocolate, chopped

Directions

1. Preheat the oven to 350°F.
2. Spread the pecan halves on a baking sheet and toast for 10 minutes, just until browned and fragrant.
3. Line two baking sheets with Silpat mats or parchment paper. Arrange clusters of 3–4 pecan halves on the baking sheets.
4. Place the caramel squares and milk in the top of a double boiler or in a medium-size saucepan. Melt the caramel over medium-low heat, stirring occasionally, until fully melted and combined. Add the sea salt; stir to combine. Remove from heat and stir in the bourbon.
5. Use a spoon to carefully pour the caramel over each nut cluster. Place the baking sheet in the fridge or freezer for a few minutes for the caramel to set.
6. Meanwhile, place the chocolate in a microwave-safe bowl. Microwave the chocolate in 30-second increments, stirring after each increment, until smooth.
7. Use a spoon to carefully pour the chocolate over the caramel clusters.
8. Let sit in the fridge or freezer for a few minutes to set.

Note: I use the Wilton Candy Melts melting pot and Wilton Candy Melts candy dipping spoon for this recipe. I think the end result looks more professional if the turtles are completely submerged in chocolate. If you know you won't make candy or chocolate-dipped strawberries often, stick to melting your chocolate in the microwave or on the stove. Don't fill up your kitchen cupboards with stuff that isn't used often.

Family Recipes

Preserving family recipes allows us to bring to our remembrance childhood memories. Passing family recipes from one generation to the next helps keep us connected. This chapter contains blank pages for you to capture your family's special dishes.

Mother Frazier's Brown Sugar Pound Cake

My grandmother, affectionately known as Ma Ruth, at one time worked as a school cafeteria cook. This recipe is not exactly a cake for a beginner, but it is worth tackling once you become comfortable in the kitchen. Now if I could just find her ambrosia salad recipe….

Mother Frazier's Brown Sugar Pound Cake

Now You're Cooking! | 157

Your Family's Special Dishes

Your Family's Special Dishes

Your Family's Special Dishes

Your Family's Special Dishes

Resources

To check out a list of Charlene's favorite recipe ingredients and potential kitchen equipment for your home, please visit www.charlenescuisine.com/nowyourecooking where you'll find easy-to-access clickable links.

Index

7Up Pound Cake 152

A

Air-Fried Chicken Livers 140, 141
Air-Fried French Fries 116, 117
Air-Fried Lemon Pepper Wings 84
Air-Fried Salmon Patties 88
Air-Fried Shrimp Hushpuppies 120
Air-Fried Sweet Potato Fries 111, 117

Amazing Italian Stuffed Peppers 78, 79
Apple and Cabbage Slaw 63
Apple Pecan Chicken Salad 62, 65
Avocado Ranch Dressing 59, 60, 61
Avocado Toast 40

B

Baked Chicken Breasts 82
Baked Chicken Thighs with Balsamic Glaze 83
Baked Potatoes 93
Baked Tomato Shells 67, 68
Baked Turkey Wings 76, 77
Banana Pudding Smoothie 20, 22, 30, 31
Banana Rum Cake 150, 151

BEVERAGES
Banana Pudding Smoothie 20, 22, 30, 31
Charlene's Front Porch Lemonade 146
Moscato Punch 122, 128, 129
Snickerdoodle Smoothie 48
Spiced Hot Chocolate 148
Strawberry Banana Smoothie 31, 32
Oreo Milkshake... 110

Bourbon Sea Salt Caramel Turtles 156

BREAKFAST
Avocado Toast 40
Banana Pudding Smoothie 20, 22, 30, 31
Breakfast Muffins 33
Country Sausage Egg Bites 34, 35
Frisky Frittata 27
McDowell's Breakfast Burrito 112, 113
Mini Toaster Waffles 38
Mrs. Hopson's Breakfast Pie 28, 29
Strawberry Banana Smoothie 31, 32
Turkey Breakfast Sausage 36, 37

C

Charlene's Front Porch Lemonade 146
Chicken Liver Pâté 138
Chicken Noodle Soup 50
Chicken Parmesan 80
Chicken Pot Pie 74
Chicken Salad in Tomato Shells 66, 67

Chicken Tortilla Soup 51
Chocolate-Dipped Oatmeal Cookies 155
Corn and Black Bean Relish 46
Country Sausage Egg Bites 34, 35
Crab Dip 44, 45
Cucumber Salad 53, 59

D

DESSERTS

7Up Pound Cake	152
Banana Rum Cake	150, 151
Bourbon Sea Salt Caramel Turtles	156
Chocolate-Dipped Oatmeal Cookies	155
Mother Frazier's Brown Sugar Pound Cake	157
Peanut Butter Oatmeal Bars	154
Snickerdoodle Smoothie	48
Sweet Potato Pie	153

DIPS

Corn and Black Bean Relish	46
Crab Dip	44, 45
Southwestern Dipping Sauce	70, 71, 72

Doritos-Crusted Chicken Tenders 70, 71

E

Easy Mac and Cheese 102, 103

F

Family Recipes 157
Flava Beans 98, 99

French Onion Soup 122, 130
Frisky Frittata 27

G

Green Beans with Almonds 94, 95

Grilled Cheese Sandwich 57, 58

H

Herbed Cream Cheese Crescent Rolls 127
Honey-Butter Corn Muffins 104

Hot Chicken Salad 73

L

Lasagna 142, 143

M

McDowell's Breakfast Burrito 112, 113
Menu 122
Mini Toaster Waffles 38
Mixed Greens with Balsamic Vinaigrette 122, 131

Moscato Punch 122, 128, 129
Mother Frazier's Brown Sugar Pound Cake .. 157
Mrs Hopson's Breakfast Pie 28, 29

O

Oreo Milkshake 31, 110

P

Parmesan-Ranch Potato Chips 42
Peanut Butter Oatmeal Bars 154

POULTRY
Air-Fried Chicken Livers 140, 141
Air-Fried Lemon Pepper Wings 91
Baked Chicken Breasts 89
Baked Chicken Thighs with Balsamic Glaze 83
Baked Turkey Wings 76, 77
Chicken Liver Pate 138, 139
Chicken Parmesan 80, 81
Chicken Pot Pie 74, 75
Doritos-Crusted Chicken Tenders 70, 71
Hot Chicken Salad 73
Roasted Chicken Breasts 136
with Lemon-Basil Sauce

R

Roasted Asparagus 106

Roasted Chicken Breasts 136
with Lemon-Basil Sauce

S

SALAD
Apple and Cabbage Slaw 63
Apple Pecan Chicken Salad 62, 65
Avocado Ranch Dressing 59, 60, 61
Chicken Salad in Tomato Shells 66, 67
Cucumber Salad 53, 59
Hot Chicken Salad 73
Savory Broccoli Salad 59, 60
Southwest Chicken Salad 64, 65

SANDWICHES
Grilled Cheese Sandwich 57, 58

Sautéed Cabbage 108
Sautéed Mushrooms and Spinach 96, 97
Savory Broccoli Salad 59, 60
Scalloped Potatoes 122, 132

SEAFOOD
Air-Fried Salmon Patties 88, 89
Air-Fried Shrimp Hushpuppies 120
Crab Dip 44
Seafood Pot Pie 87
Shrimp Fried Rice 121
Shrimp Teriyaki Stir-Fry 118, 119
Tuna Pasta 90, 91
Tuna Salad 86

Seafood Pot Pie 87
Seven Up Pound Cake 152
Sexy Meatloaf with Brown Sugar Glaze 144, 145
Shrimp Fried Rice 121
Shrimp Teriyaki Stir-Fry 118, 119
Simply Delicious Apple Dump Cake 134

SIDES

Air-Fried French Fries 116, 117
Air-Fried Sweet Potato Fries 111, 117
Easy Mac and Cheese 102, 103
Flava Beans 98, 99
Herbed Cream Cheese Crescent Rolls 127
Green Beans with Almonds 94, 95
Honey Butter Corn Muffins 104
Mixed Greens with Balsamic Vinaigrette 122, 131
Roasted Asparagus 106
Sauteed Cabbage 108
Sauteed Mushrooms and Spinach 96, 97
Scalloped Potatoes 122, 132, 133
Smoky Greens 105
Steamed Zucchini and Yellow Squash 100, 101
Yellow Rice 107
Oreo Milkshake... 110
Simply Delicious Apple Dump Cake .. 122, 134
Snickerdoodle Smoothie 31, 48

SOUP

Chicken Noodle 50
Chicken Tortilla 51
French Onion 122, 130
Sweet Potato and Apple Bisque 54, 55
Tasty Turkey Chili 52
Tomato 56, 57

Southwest Chicken Salad 64, 65
Southwestern Dipping Sauce 70, 71, 72
Southwestern Egg Rolls 114, 115
Spiced Hot Chocolate 148
Strawberry Banana Smoothie 31, 32
Sweet Potato and Apple Bisque 54, 55
Sweet Potato Pie 153

T

Tasty Turkey Chili 52
Thanksgiving Crescent Rolls 43
Tomato Soup 56, 57
Tuna Pasta 90, 91

Tuna Salad 86
Turkey Breakfast Sausage 36, 37
Turkey Pepperoni and Sausage Pizza Pockets 47

Y

Yellow Rice 107